THE
RITUAL REASON WHY

BY
CHARLES WALKER

EDITED AND REVISED BY
T. I. BALL, LL.D.

"What mean ye by this Service"
Exod. xii. 26

WIPF & STOCK · Eugene, Oregon

Wipf and Stock Publishers
199 W 8th Ave, Suite 3
Eugene, OR 97401

The Ritual Reason Why
By Walker, Charles and Bell, T. I.
ISBN 13: 978-1-62032-141-6
Publication date 3/1/2012
Previously published by A. R. Mowbray, 1868

INDEX TO SECTIONS

		PAGE
I.	INTRODUCTORY	1
II.	THE ARRANGEMENT AND ORNAMENTS OF THE CHURCH, par. 10-54	6
III.	ORNAMENTS OF THE MINISTERS, par. 55-109	18
IV.	BENEDICTIONS, par. 110-36	33
V.	FEASTS AND FASTS, par. 137-85	41
VI.	MATINS AND EVENSONG, par. 186-256	53
VII.	SOLEMN TE DEUM, par. 257-59	78
VIII.	THE LITANY, par. 260-62	79
IX.	PROCESSIONS, par. 263-73	81
X.	LOW CELEBRATION, par. 274-409	86
XI.	HIGH OR SOLEMN CELEBRATION, par. 410-50	145
XII.	FUNERAL AND MORTUARY CELEBRATIONS, par. 451-66	159
XIII.	THE OCCASIONAL SERVICES, par. 467-501	164
XIV.	CEREMONIES PECULIAR TO CERTAIN SEASONS, par. 502-55	175

APPENDIX

XV.	THE CANONICAL HOURS, par. 556-99	198
INDEX		215

"And here is to be noted that such Ornaments of the Church, and of the ministers thereof, at all times of their Ministration, shall be retained, and be in use, as were in this Church of *England*, by the authority of Parliament, in the Second Year of the Reign of King *Edward* the Sixth."—*Rubric in the Book of Common Prayer.*

" Whosoever through his private judgement, willingly and purposely, doth openly break the traditions and ceremonies of the Church, which be not repugnant to the Word of God, and be ordained and approved by common authority, ought to be rebuked openly (that others may fear to do the like), as he that offendeth against the common order of the Church."—*Article* **xxxiv.**

THE RITUAL 'REASON WHY'

"*What mean ye by this Service?*"

SECTION I

1. *What is Ritual?*

It is the employment of symbols in Divine worship according to a recognized or traditional system.

2. *To what end are symbols thus employed?*

Partly to uphold the dignity of Divine worship; and partly to shadow forth by outward deed and gesture certain truths, which might otherwise be lost sight of. In other words: for the glory of God and the edification of His people.

3. *How is God glorified by symbolic worship?*

In many ways. Because He is the God of truth, He is glorified by that which is the representative and guardian of truth. Because He is the Lord and Creator of all, He is fitly honoured by that which employs not merely the *intellect*, but the *senses*, not merely the *soul*, but the *body* of His children; and by which the inanimate creation is pressed into the service of the sanctuary. Because He is the God of Order, He is glorified by that which ensures *care*, even about the comparative trifles of His service, and which precludes slovenliness. While, as the Giver of all good things, He is fitly honoured by symbols which are more or less of a *costly* nature.

4. Is this view Scriptural?

Yes. The minute directions given under the old Law about the types and symbols to be employed in the Tabernacle show that God was glorified by ceremonies which as the shadows of things to come were the outward signs of spiritual truth: and that He willed to be worshipped by the bodily senses not less than by the spirit: while the case of David, who "would not offer to the Lord his God of that which did cost him nothing," and the direction that His people were not to appear empty before the Lord, show that a *costly* worship was sanctioned by God and was acceptable to Him.

5. This was under the Old Law: can you adduce instances from the New Testament?

Certainly. We have the express declaration of our Lord that He came not to *destroy* the law but to *fulfil* it. He Himself was a frequent attendant at the Temple services. He constantly employed symbolic acts in His public ministry, as when He anointed the blind man with spittle, when He washed the disciples' feet, etc. And in instituting the Sacraments He made certain acts and gestures and certain bodily elements the channels by which He would confer His grace.

6. *Do you find this system continued by the Apostles?*

We do. The disciples continued to attend the Temple services, and were constant in "the breaking of the Bread and in the prayers."[1] So too the Apostles *baptized* those that were converted; and *laid their hands* on those that were to receive the Holy Ghost or to be set apart for the ministry. And we find S. Paul giving directions for the proper administration of the Lord's Supper, and promising to set the rest in order when he came. The same Apostle, to whom was committed the care of all the Churches, was most careful that "all things should be done decently and in order"[2]

7. *Can you give me any further instances?*

There is the case of the woman that anointed the feet of our Lord with precious ointment, when Judas took exception to the *costly character*

---

[1] Acts ii. 42: τῇ κλάσει τοῦ ἄρτου καὶ ταῖς προσευχαῖς, i.e. the Eucharistic breaking of bread, and the accompanying prayers. Such set forms or liturgies were of earliest date; so much so that S. Paul quotes from one: 1 Cor. ii. 9. Compare Liturgy of S. James. [Scholars do not generally admit this supposed quotation. B.]

[2] 1 Cor. xiv. 40: κατὰ τάξιν, according to (accustomed) form.

of this act of service. I may add also that it has been maintained that the "cloke" which S. Paul left at Troas was the Eucharistic vestment, the "parchments" he speaks of being the Liturgy:[1] and that the Apostle John is believed to have borrowed his imagery of the heavenly worship from that which was then customary in the Church.[2]

8. *Does ecclesiastical history support this view?*

Yes: the fact that the Eastern and Western Churches, differing so widely as they do in language, in the customs of their people, and in many minor points of ceremonial, should yet employ a system of symbolism in worship, essentially the same in all its broad principles, is in itself a proof. Nor is other wanting. Lights and incense are mentioned in the early liturgies. Even in the times of persecution, when Christians had to worship in dens and caves of the earth, the worship of God was conducted with splendour and costliness. Thus the historian Eusebius tells us that the magnificence of the sacred vessels inflamed the cupidity of the persecutors, as was the case with S. Lawrence, who suffered martyrdom A.D. 258, because he would not give up the treasures of the Church. S. Optatus testifies that in the Diocletian persecution the churches had very many

---

[1] 2 Tim. iv. 13: φελόνην, which is still the word employed in the Eastern liturgies to denote the chasuble.

[2] Revelation, *passim*.

ornaments of gold and silver. Prudentius thus speaks of the ornaments of the Church in Rome when S. Lawrence was martyred, " The Priests offer in gold; the sacred Blood is received in silver chalices; in the nightly sacrifices the wax tapers are fixed in golden candlesticks." It is certain that as soon as the conversion of Constantine gave peace to the Church Divine Worship was at once celebrated with great pomp and magnificence; and it is noticeable that Eusebius in speaking of the restoration of the churches, and the dedication of new ones which then ensued, has handed down a sermon of his own, in which he speaks of S. Paulinus, Bishop of Tyre, who had engaged himself in this work as "a new Bezaleel," of whom we read (*Exod.* xxxv. 35), that God filled him with wisdom of heart to work all manner of works of the engraver, and of the cunning workman, *and of the embroiderer*, in blue and in purple, and in scarlet, and in fine linen. In a word, it is not too much to say that till the sixteenth century no Christian Church was deficient in the three leading characteristics of ritual— vestments, lights, and incense.

9. As it does not enter into the scope of the present work to do more than glance at the historical evidence in favour of Ritual, the inquiring reader is referred to *The Ritual of the New Testament*, by the Rev. T. E. Bridgett (Burns & Oates), which, though written from a Roman Catholic point of view, contains little that a consistent English Catholic need except against.

SECTION II

THE ARRANGEMENT AND ORNAMENTS OF THE CHURCH

10. *What are the chief ornaments of the church?*

The font, which is used in the administration of Baptism, and the altar, which serves for the celebration of the Holy Communion. To these may be added the pulpit, and the seats in the chancel for the choir.

11. *I notice that the font is generally placed near the west door. Why is this?*

To show that Baptism is the gate by which we enter into the fold of Christ's Church.

12. *Why is the portion reserved for the choir marked off from the rest of the church by being raised, and sometimes by a screen?*

Because as the body of the church signifies the Church Militant, the choir is typical of the Church Triumphant in heaven. The screen represents the gate of death, by which we enter into heavenly rest.

13. *Is not this screen generally surmounted by a cross? Why is this?*

To show that it is by the Passion and Death

of Christ alone that we can gain an entrance into heaven.

14. *Why is the altar generally placed at the east end of the church?*

In token that Christ is the true Sun of Righteousness; for which reason it is a prevalent custom in the Church to worship towards the point where the sun rises.

15. *The altar, I perceive, is railed off from the chancel. Why is this?*

Partly from motives of reverence; partly because the sanctuary is symbolical of the Holy of Holies, into which the Priest entered to plead for the people, or rather of that innermost heaven where our Great High Priest hath entered through the veil of His flesh, and where He ever maketh intercession for us, pleading the merits of His all-perfect Sacrifice.

16. *Why is the altar made so conspicuous?*

Because it is the holiest part of the church.

17. *How so?*

It is used in the highest act of Divine worship, the Holy Eucharist in which by the ministry of His Church the Eternal Son of God offers His Death and Passion to His Father. It is raised because our Lord suffered on the *Mount*; and is made of wood as representing the Cross; or of stone as symbolical of the rock of Calvary.

18. *Why is the front of the altar covered with a veil or hanging?*

From motives of respect, and in order to mark the various seasons of the Church by hangings of different colours.

19. *What are these colours?*

They are generally these five; white, red, violet, green, and black. But according to Old English use, blue, brown, grey, and yellow were also employed.

20. *How do you account for the employment of these colours?*

They fitly set forth, in the symbolism of colour, the character of the days and seasons for which they are employed. [B.]

21. *Why is the altar surmounted by a cross?*

To remind us of the Death of Christ, which is especially shown forth in the Holy Eucharist.

22. *There are other ornaments of the altar besides the hangings and cross. Will you explain them?*

There are two lights which burn at the time of the celebration, to signify that Christ is the true light of the world; and to represent His two natures, the Human and the Divine, both which He bears at the Right Hand of the Father in heaven. Other lights are lit round and about the altar in festal seasons as a sign of spiritual joy, as S. Jerome testifies. The altar is also decked with flowers for the same reason, and in honour of Him Who is the Rose of Sharon and the Lily of the Valley. All these are not placed on the altar proper (which is reserved for the sacred vessels directly employed in the offering of the Eucharistic Sacrifice), but on one or more shelves or steps, called the *retable*, and sometimes, but improperly, the *super-altar*.[1] There is also a covering of silk, usually crimson, called the super-frontal, and a fair linen cloth covering the top and sides, and marked with five crosses.

23. *Why is the super-frontal generally crimson?*

As symbolical of the Blood-shedding of our Lord. For a similar reason the fair linen cloth, which represents the winding-sheet in which the dead Body of our Saviour was wrapped at His Burial, is marked with five crosses as a memento of His five wounds.

24. *Is there any other furniture appointed for the sanctuary?*

Yes; there are the credence, and the sedilia or seats for the clergy.

---

[1] The "super-altar" is a small portable slab of stone, which is placed on altars which lack a stone mensa, or have not been consecrated. In the East a linen napkin, which has been blessed by the Bishop, answers the purpose.

25. *What is the credence?*

It is a table at which the elements are prepared

26. *Why is this done at the credence?*

Partly for convenience, partly out of reverence, so that the altar may be entirely reserved for the actual offering of the Holy Sacrifice; and in order that the elements may not be placed upon the altar before the oblation.

27. *When are the sedilia employed?*

When the officiants have occasion to be seated during the celebration. The celebrant occupies the seat nearest the altar, the deacon the next, then the subdeacon. Or else the celebrant sits in the midst, the deacon at his right hand, the subdeacon at his left.

28. *What is the meaning of this arrangement?*

To mark the different degrees of dignity in those engaged in the service.

29. *Are there not other ornaments of the church besides those you have mentioned?*

Yes: for the altar there are the book-desk and service book for the celebrant; the paten, chalice, chalice-veil, corporal, and burse; for the credence, cruets, pyx or canister for the altar-breads, bason, napkin, and alms-dish; before the altar, two standard lights, in some churches lecterns for the Epistle and Gospel;

in the choir, lectern for the antiphons; in the nave, pulpit, litany-desk, lectern for the lessons. In addition to these may be mentioned the censer or thurible, acolytes' candlesticks, processional cross and banners, sanctus-bell, triptych or altar-piece; bier with pall for funerals; houselling-cloth, and baptismal shell.

30. *What is the paten?*

A thin disk of gold or silver gilt, on which the altar breads are placed for consecration, and from which the people are communicated.

31. *Are the people always communicated from the paten?*

Sometimes the ciborium is used instead.

32. *What is the ciborium?*

A kind of shallow cup or chalice with a cover to it.

Where the Sacrament is reserved for the sick the ciborium is also used for that purpose. The bottom of the bowl is slightly elevated inside to enable the sacred particles to be readily removed.

33. *What is the chalice?*

The sacramental cup in which the wine is consecrated, and from which the people are communicated.

34. *What is the chalice-veil?*

A square of silk embroidered and fringed,

varying in colour according to the season. It is used for covering the chalice when empty.

35. In the old English rite it was also used by the acolyte to wrap the paten in when held by him in certain parts of the service. This rite is now obsolete.

36. *What is the corporal?*

A napkin of fine linen spread on the altar at the time of the Eucharistic service. The chalice is placed on the centre of it, and the paten in front of the chalice. When the altar-breads are on the altar the lower right-hand corner of the corporal is turned back over them, except during the oblation and consecration.

According to the old English rite the corporal is made sufficiently large for a fold of it to turn over and cover the chalice; when this is not the case, the pall, a piece of cardboard about eight inches square with linen on either side, is alone used to cover the chalice till after the communication of the people, when a second corporal, somewhat smaller and edged with lace, is placed over the chalice till the ablutions.

37. *What is the burse?*

The burse (or *corporas case*, as it used to be called in England) is a kind of pocket, formed of two squares of thick card, covered with silk, and so arranged as to open at the end. In the pocket so formed the corporals and pall are kept when not in use. In texture, colour, and embroidery the burse corresponds with the chalice-veil. It is brought in on the top of the veiled chalice, and when empty during the celebration stands upright against the retable.

38. *What are the cruets?*

Vessels of glass or metal, one of which contains the wine to be used for the celebration of the Eucharist; the other the water for mixing therewith, and also for the washing of the priest's hands. The dish in which they stand often serves for the basin at the last-mentioned rite.

39. Two spoons are frequently used in addition to the cruets; one of which the priest uses for measuring out the small quantity of water to be mixed with the wine; the other (which has a perforated bowl) he uses (if need be) for removing a fly or other impurity from the chalice.

40. *What is the pyx?*

A metal canister in which the altar-breads are kept till required for use.

Pyx is also the name given to a similar canister of precious metal, in which the Blessed Sacrament is reserved in place of the ciborium, and to a smaller canister in which it was conveyed to the sick. In the former case it was usually distinguished from the canister for altar-breads both by the costliness of its make and by the words " Corpus Domini " engraved round it. In the old English rite the Sacrament was reserved in a pyx suspended over the altar. In the modern Roman Church it is placed in the tabernacle.

41. *For what are the bason and napkin?*

For the lavabo or washing of the priest's hands. The rim of the bason is sometimes engraved with an appropriate inscription, such as "I will wash mine hands in innocency, O Lord."

42. *What is the piscina?*

A small stone bason formed in the east wall at the Epistle end of the altar. Anciently the priest used it for the lavabo in place of a bason. The water in which any sacred vessel or ornament has been washed is also poured into the piscina, which is furnished with a drain for the purpose of carrying away any such fluids.

43. *What are lecterns?*

Large desks of brass or wood to hold certain of the large service books. Those most frequently in use in England are for reading the lessons from, and are sometimes placed outside and sometimes within the choir screen. They are frequently made in the shape of an eagle. In addition to the lectern for the lessons, one is sometimes placed in the midst of the choir for the rulers to sing the antiphons and intone the commencement of the Psalms, etc., from; and two below the altar-steps for the Epistle and Gospel.

44. *For what are the two standard lights before the altar?*

For use in solemn Vespers or Matins, and at solemn celebrations of the Holy Eucharist.

The old English rite prescribes four lights for each of these occasions, two upon and two below the altar. In the Roman rite the standard lights are lighted at High Mass before the Canon.

45. *Are there any other special lights?*

There are the lenten-hearse and the paschal taper.

46. *What is the lenten-hearse?*

The lenten or tenebrae-hearse is a triangular stand, containing thirteen (or according to English use twenty-four) candles. They are used at Matins on Maundy Thursday, Good Friday, and Holy Saturday. They are extinguished one by one as the Psalms are recited, in token of that great darkness which was upon the earth during our Lord's Passion, and also of our Lord's abiding three days in the grave.

47. *What is the paschal taper?*

It is a large candle placed on the Gospel side of the altar during the Easter season. It burns throughout Easter week at Matins, Evensong, and the Eucharist, thence on all Sundays, Holy Days, and up to the Ascension at the Eucharist only. It symbolizes our Lord's presence with His disciples during the forty days after the Resurrection. On Ascension Day it is extinguished at the Gospel (which tells of His Ascension), in token that the light of His visible presence on earth was then removed. The tall stand for the paschal taper is called the *paschal candlestick*, or *paschal-post*.

48. *What is the censer?*

The censer, or thurible, is a vessel of brass or silver, in which incense is offered. It is usually in the shape of a cup, with a perforated cover, through which the fumes of the incense escape, and is carried by three chains attached to the bowl, whilst a fourth serves to raise the cover when required.

49. *What are the acolytes' candlesticks?*

Brass candlesticks, somewhat smaller than those on the altar, and having triangular stands. They are carried by the acolytes in processions; at the Gospel and some other parts of the Holy Eucharist; and at the *Magnificat* (or *Benedictus*) and Collect in solemn service.

50. *What is the processional cross?*

A tall wand of wood or metal, surmounted by a cross, borne at the head of processions; before the deacon when he sings the Gospel on festivals; and at other times.

The processional cross and banners will be fully explained in the section on processions.

51. *What is a triptych?*

It is a painting on a sort of tablet in three divisions, made to open and shut, the two outer folding over the centre when closed. Triptychs

ORNAMENTS OF THE CHURCH 17

are frequently placed behind the cross on the retable to form an altar-piece. Sculptured pieces are usually called the *reredos*; tapestry, or hangings behind the altar, the *dossal*.

52. *What is the sanctus-bell?*

It is a small bell, either placed on the altar-steps or hung in a small gable over the chancel, and rung at the sanctus to give notice that the canon or most solemn part of the service is about to commence, and at the consecration to inform the people that the Eucharistic mystery is accomplished, and to stir up their devotion.

53. *What is the houselling-cloth?*

A long napkin, either spread over the altar-rails or held before the communicants to guard against any particle of the Blessed Sacrament falling to the ground.

54. *What is the baptismal-shell?*

It is a small metal vessel in the shape of a scallop-shell used for taking up the water from the font and pouring it over the head of the person to be baptized. Sometimes real shells polished, and having some sacred subject engraved on them, are used.

SECTION III

ORNAMENTS OF THE MINISTERS

55. *Those who occupy the choir are vested in white. Will you explain the reason?*

I have already said that the chancel is symbolical of heaven. Those who occupy it, as being more directly engaged in the services of God, are clothed in fine linen, which as representing the righteousness of Saints is described by S. John as the vesture of the Church Triumphant—the Bride of Christ (*Rev.* xix. 8).

56. *The surplice, then, is the ordinary choir dress?*

Yes: it is worn over the cassock, which is the distinguishing mark of all engaged in God's service.

57. *What do these dresses signify?*

The cassock, which entirely hides the ordinary dress, is emblematical of the spirit of recollection and devotion which becomes those who serve in the sanctuary: while the surplice represents the innocency of life and purity of heart without which our service will not be acceptable to God.

58. *Will you describe the cassock to me more in detail?*

The cassock is a long coat buttoning over the breast and reaching to the feet. It is confined at the waist by a broad sash called the *cincture*. The collar is made to fasten right round the throat.

59. The cassock is ordinarily *black*, and signifies separation from the world.[1] The Bishop's cassock is *violet*, a colour which signifies rule or authority. According to old English use, doctors of divinity wear *scarlet* cassocks. The choir-boys' cassocks differ considerably in colour. In addition to black, blue, scarlet, and purple are frequently used. Where there are two sets, scarlet cassocks are generally used for ordinary Sundays and feasts; blue, black, or purple for weekdays, Advent, Lent, etc. According to an eminent ritualist, the choristers' cassocks should be ordinarily black; scarlet in churches which are *royal* foundations;[2] purple in *Episcopal* foundations; and perhaps blue in churches dedicated in honour of the Blessed Virgin, but, however sound in theory, this does not seem to be generally adhered to in practice in any part of the Church.

60. *What is the surplice?*

A vestment of linen, shorter and fuller than the cassock. The arms are of considerable width at the wrists, and there is an aperture at

---

[1] In some parts of the Eastern Church cassocks of *brown*, or other sober hue, are used by the clergy. Members of religious orders wear the habit of their order in place of the cassock.

[2] The choristers of the Chapel Royal wear scarlet and gold uniforms.

the neck of sufficient size to enable the wearer to pass it over his head.

61. *Is there any other dress used in the choir?*

Yes; there are two varieties of the surplice not uncommonly to be met with, the cotta and the rochet.

62. *What is the cotta?*

The cotta is much shorter than the surplice, and is either entirely wanting in sleeves, or has short ones reaching to a little below the elbow. The bottom of the cotta and the ends of the sleeves are frequently edged with lace, an ornamentation which corresponds with the "apparels" of the alb.

63. *What is the rochet?*

The rochet is a short alb, generally made of lawn, or fine linen. Both these varieties of the surplice have resulted from the inconvenience of the wide pendant sleeves of the *surplice proper* in certain functions, such as the administration of Baptism, when the sleeves were apt to get wetted, and in serving at the Holy Eucharist at times when the alb would be out of place.

64. The *rochet* is also worn by bishops in place of the surplice.

65. *Are not the girded alb and the cope sometimes employed in choir?*

Yes; on the more solemn occasions.

66. *What is the alb?*

A linen vestment much longer than the surplice, and with tight sleeves like those of the cassock. It is confined at the waist by a girdle or sash.

67. *When is this vestment worn in choir?*

In many parts of the Church it is employed in solemn celebrations of the Holy Eucharist; also by the "ministers," that is, the acolytes and thurifer, at solemn Matins and Evensong.

68. *Why?*

Because the choir are engaged in assisting the priest in the offering of the sacrifice. Hence they wear the alb, which is the sacrificial vestment.

69. *What is the cope?*

A large semicircular cloak of silk or other stuff, fastening in front by a clasp or morse. The straight piece is usually ornamented with a broad orphrey or strip of embroidery, the circular edge with a narrow. At the back is a piece of embroidery in the shape of a shield, called the *hood*.

70. *How is the cope employed?*

It is worn over the alb or surplice by the priest in procession and at solemn Vespers or Matins;[1] by the rulers of the choir, and by the bishop in certain ministrations.

---

[1] According to old English use the priest does not assume the cope till the *Magnificat* or *Benedictus*.

71. *Of what is it symbolical?*

It is symbolical of rule, and is therefore worn by those who have dignity in the choir. It is not an Eucharistic but a choral vestment.

72. *Are there other choir habits?*

Yes; when the cope is not used the choral tippet, or the hood, and sometimes the stole, are worn.

73. *What is the choral tippet?*

A cape of black silk or stuff worn over the surplice, and reaching about half-way between the elbow and wrist.

74. *What is the hood?*

It differs from the tippet in colour, which varies according to the University and degree of the wearer; and is furnished at the back with a small hood, whence it derives its name.

75. *What is the stole?*

A narrow strip of silk passed over the neck, and hanging in front to about the knees of the wearer. It is usually ornamented with a cross at the neck and at either extremity. The ends are slightly expanded and fringed. It varies in colour (as does the cope) with the season.

76. *What are the Eucharistic vestments?*

The amice, alb, girdle, stole, maniple, tunic, dalmatic, and chasuble.

ORNAMENTS OF THE MINISTERS 23

77. Why are special vestments assigned to the Eucharist?

To mark the dignity of the service, and as symbolical of the Passion of Christ, which is therein commemorated.

78. Whence did the Church derive them?

Partly from the ordinary dress of apostolic times (preserving, however, a Syrian type out of reverence to the earthly life of her Lord): partly perhaps from the ceremonial robes in use in the ancient world.

79. What is the amice?

A square piece of linen which is first placed on the head, and then, being fastened round the neck, is turned back to form a kind of collar.

80. What is its symbolical meaning?

It is interpreted as representing the linen rag wherewith the Jews blindfolded our Saviour; also as a type of the helmet of salvation, wherewith the good soldier of Jesus Christ is equipped.

81. What is the alb?

I have already described it as differing from the surplice in its greater length, and in the tightness of its sleeves. It is also generally made of finer linen; and, as employed in the Eucharist, is ornamented with embroidery at the foot, before and behind, and at the sleeves. These patches of embroidery are called the *apparels*.

82. *Of what is the alb symbolical?*

It is, like the surplice, emblematical of purity and innocence, as also of the ministerial office (1 *Sam.* ii. 18; *Rev.* xv. 6). It is also held to represent the white garment[1] in which Herod clothed our Saviour.

83. *What is the girdle?*

A white cord used to confine the alb at the waist.

84. *By whom are the amice, alb, and girdle worn?*

By the priest, deacon, and subdeacon, and the other "ministers," that is, the acolytes and thurifer. The latter, however, generally substitute for the girdle a broad sash of the colour of their cassocks, and not unfrequently substitute lace on the bottom of the alb for apparels.

85. *What is the maniple?*

It is in shape like the stole, but much smaller, and is worn by the priest, deacon, and subdeacon over their left arm.

---

[1] In S. Luke xxiii. 11, the Vulgate reads "white" for 'gorgeous."

86. *How is the stole worn in the Eucharist?*

The celebrant wears it crossed over his breast; the deacon fastens it on his left shoulder, and crossing it over his breast secures the ends under his right arm. The subdeacon does not wear it.

87. *What do these represent?*

The girdle is emblematic of the work of the Lord; to perform which the sacred ministers gird up as it were their loins: also of continence. The maniple is interpreted as an emblem of sorrow for sin. The stole represents the yoke of Christ, and is worn by the deacon over one shoulder only, as a sign of the subordination of his office. Lastly, all these are taken to represent the cords and fetters with which the officers bound Jesus.

88. *What is the principal vestment of the priest?*

The chasuble: an oval garment without sleeves, open at the sides, having an aperture at the neck through which he passes his head.

89. *What is the symbolic meaning of the chasuble?*

It represents the seamless vest of Christ; as also the purple garment, after being endued with which He was made to carry His Cross. It is also emblematic of charity.

90. *The chasuble, I observe, is embroidered with a cross on the back and a plain stripe in front. Why is this?*

The cross is symbolical of that which our Lord carried up the hill of Calvary; the stripe, of the pillar at which He was scourged. It reminds the priest that he must carry his cross after Christ, and must ever lean on Him as his true support.

91. In many parts of the Church, and especially in England, the chasuble has a cross in front as well as behind. To this custom Thomas à Kempis refers in the *Imitation of Christ* (Bk. iv, ch. 5): " Before him he (i.e. the priest) beareth his cross on the chasuble, that he may diligently behold the footsteps of Christ, and fervently endeavour to follow after them. Behind him he is marked with the cross that he may mildly suffer for God's sake whatsoever adversities befall him from others. He weareth the cross before that he may bewail his own sins, and behind that he may lament the sins of others, and know that he standeth in the midst betwixt God and the sinner." The transverse beams of these crosses are generally placed at an acute instead of a right angle with the shaft (thus Ψ); as this was the form taken by our Lord's arms when extended on the cross. The *Y-Cross*, as it is called, thus reminds us of that *lifting up of His hands* (Ps. cxli. 2), which, first on Calvary, and now by way of representation on the altars of the Christian Church, is the true and acceptable Sacrifice.

92. *What are the principal vestments of the deacon and subdeacon?*

Of the deacon the dalmatic; of the subdeacon the tunic. These vestments vary very slightly in form. The dalmatic is somewhat fuller and longer, and is generally more richly ornamented.

93. *What do these garments typify?*

They represent the ministerial office; it being the duty of the deacon to minister to the priest, and the subdeacon to the deacon.

94. *Do the deacon and subdeacon always use these vestments?*

No; sometimes they minister in the planeta, or folded chasuble; or in albs and amices only.

95. *Why is this?*

Because the dalmatic and tunic are considered as festal garments, and so are not used in penitential seasons.

96. *What are these seasons?*

Advent and the season between Septuagesima and Easter[1] which includes the Lent fast; the four Ember seasons; the Rogation days; and the vigils of saints' days and festivals.

97. *Is the planeta always used then?*

No; sometimes the church is poor in vestments, and then the deacon and subdeacon minister in their albs at these times, which they

---

[1] According to Sarum use, the dalmatic and tunic are to be used on feasts falling at these times, although the *Te Deum* is not said.

do according to old English use under any circumstances on Good Friday, the Rogation days, and in ferial celebrations for the dead.

98. *Are there any exceptions to these rules?*

Yes; the Vigils of Christmas, Easter, and Pentecost, and the Ember days in Whitsun week.

99. *Are there any other observances connected with these penitential times?*

Yes; the *Te Deum* is omitted at Matins. Formerly the *Gloria in Excelsis* also was omitted in the Eucharist.

100. *You said that the stole varied in colour with the season. Is this the case with the other vestments?*

The maniple, chasuble, dalmatic, tunic, and cope vary in the same manner.

101. *Will you explain these variations in colour?*

These vestments are *White* on all the great festivals of our Lord, of the Blessed Virgin, and of all Saints who did not suffer martyrdom; white being the colour appropriated to joy, and signifying purity. *Red* is used on the feasts of martyrs, typifying that they shed their blood for the testimony of Jesus; also on the feasts of the Holy Cross—that cross which was anointed with the Blood of the Lamb; and at Whitsuntide, when the Holy Ghost descended in the likeness of tongues of fire. *Violet* is the penitential colour, and is used in Advent, Lent, Vigils, etc. *Green* is the colour for Sundays and weekdays falling within no special season, as being the prevailing colour of nature. *Black* is made use of at funerals, and on Good Friday.

102. *Are these colours always observed?*

No; many churches do not possess complete sets of vestments, and in others what some think to be the old English colours are followed.

103. *What are these?*

They are the same as those above, but worn in a slightly different order, and with the addition of brown, grey, blue, and yellow.

104. *Will you explain to me this order?*

Willingly. According to this use, *Red* is used on all Sundays throughout the year, except from Easter to Pentecost, unless a festival supercedes the Sunday services. The same colour serves for Ash Wednesday, Good Friday, Maundy Thursday, and Easter and Whitsun eves. *White* is employed throughout Eastertide (i.e. from Easter to Whitsun Eve), whether the service be of Sunday, of a Saint's day, or of the feria, with the exception of the Invention of the Cross (May 3). *Yellow* is employed for the feasts of confessors. *Blue* is used indifferently with green as the ferial colour; and *Brown* or *Grey* with violet for penitential times.

105. *Red*, in this rite, is used in a twofold aspect; as a solemnly penitential colour (hence its use on Ash Wednesday and the last three days of Holy Week), and as an ordinary Dominical colour; in the first case in order to connect all our penitence with the Passion of Christ, teaching us to mourn for our sins, not merely because they have injured us, but chiefly because they "have crucified the Son of God afresh"; in the second, because Sunday is the weekly feast of Him Who is the King of Martyrs. It serves also for Whitsuntide, the feasts of martyrs, and of the cross, for the reason given above. *Yellow* is symbolical of that "robe of glory" with which those who have confessed the Name of Jesus are clothed. *Blue*, the colour of the firmament, is fitly employed for the weekdays after Trinity, the season which represents the everlasting rest that remaineth to the people of God; and thence came to be used for the few similar days after Epiphany. *Brown* and *Grey*, as expressive of the "sackcloth" of mourning and penitence, are assigned for weekday use in penitential seasons.

106. While certain colours (hence called the *liturgical colours*) are employed in a certain order for symbolical purposes, in the embroidery and trimming of the above vestments, and in the general decoration of churches, all colours are employed at the dictation of taste, to His glory Who created the many hues of nature, and gave to man the power of seeing, and deriving pleasure from them.

107. *What is the " biretta" ?*

A square cap of black silk or other stuff, worn by persons in Holy Orders at processions and other out-door functions.

ORNAMENTS OF THE MINISTERS

108. The *biretta* is the non-episcopal form of the *mitre*, and both signify the helmet of salvation and the glory of the Priesthood. The mitre is cloven in the midst, like the "tongues of fire" which fell upon the Apostles (*Acts* ii. 3) to show that the wearer is a successor of the Apostles, and shares with them in the Pentecostal gift. It is a question whether the use of the mitre is of extreme antiquity. Some even assign its introduction to the tenth century. But Bona (*Rer. Lit.* lib. i, c. xxiv), while admitting the possibility of the fact, shows that *some* ornament of the head was worn from the earliest ages. The reader will remember that under the old law a "mitre" (or turban) of fine linen was appointed for the high priest (*Exod.* xxviii. 4), and "bonnets" for the priests and Levites (*v.* 40). The fathers mention that S. James the Just, first Bishop of Jerusalem, and also the Apostle S. John, were in the habit of wearing the golden plate which was prescribed for the mitre of the high priest in the Jewish ritual.

In the Eastern Church the actual mitre is unknown, but the clergy wear a particular kind of cap, over which they arrange the hood.

109. *Are not both the episcopal mitre and the biretta frequently worn in church?*

Yes. The universality of the practice shows that the injunction of S. Paul (1 *Cor.* xi. 4) either referred *alone* to the particular acts of "praying" and "prophesying," or were mainly directed against the uncomeliness of a woman entering the assembly of the faithful with uncovered head (*v.* 15). The bishop wears the mitre in the acts of Confirmation and conferring Orders, but lays it aside when engaged in prayer; the biretta is worn on entering and leaving church, and in some parts of the church during the singing of the Psalms. Members of religious orders use the *hood* of their habit (sometimes, but improperly, called the *cowl*) in place of the biretta.[1]

NOTE.—The account given, pp. 28–30, of the so-called "Old English" colours is left as the author wrote it; but it must be borne in mind that antiquarians and liturgists are by no means agreed among themselves as to many details connected with the liturgical use of colours in the pre-reformation Church of England; what we learn from the rubrics and ancient records is incomplete, and in some instances contradictory. The account here given by Mr. Walker is probably as near, or as wide of, the mark as any others given by any one else.

With regard to the wearing of the biretta, or square cap, in church, it should not be forgotten that there is no evidence to show that such a custom existed in the pre-reformation Church of England, nor perhaps anciently in France, or Flanders; the custom is probably Italian in origin (and is none the worse for that in itself), but it is more fussy than dignified; as has been remarked, the one reason why a biretta is worn in church seems to be that it may be taken off. If so, why not take it off before going into church? [B.]

---

[1] The cowl is a loose vestment, worn over the *frock* in the winter season and during the night office. The other parts of the monastic or religious habit are: the *scapular*, a narrow strip of serge or other stuff, covering the shoulders and hanging before and behind down to between the knee and the hem of the frock; and the *girdle* or *rope*, which is generally ornamented with three knots, signifying the three vows of poverty, chastity, and obedience; and (in some orders) the *sandals*.

SECTION IV

BENEDICTIONS

110. *Is it not customary to set apart the various "ornaments of the church, and of the ministers thereof," for the service of God by a form of benediction?*

Yes; the natural instincts of piety and the requirements of God Himself under the old law, as well as the universal custom of the Church in all ages, alike point to the propriety of so doing.

111. *Is there not also a theological reason for the custom?*

Yes; the creation having been put under a curse on account of man's fall, shares also in its degree in the blessings of man's redemption. But as the blessings of that redemption are conveyed to man by means of sacraments, so they are conveyed to the lower creation by the Church's benedictions.

112. *Why is water blessed?*

Before baptism in order to set apart the element to the service of God in the administration of that sacrament; before it is poured into the chalice at the Holy Eucharist for the same reason; at other times to put the people in remembrance of their baptism and to convey to them the Church's benediction in the absence of a minister.

113. *Will you explain the last reason?*

The priest in blessing the water sets it apart for the use of the people and prays God to give His blessing to all who use it.

114. It is a very ancient custom for the people to sign themselves on entering and leaving church with water so blessed, thus reminding themselves that they were set apart to God's service in Holy Baptism, and also of the need of inward purity if they would give themselves aright to His worship. Alexander I, Bishop of Rome, speaks of it in A.D. 109, in terms which show him to be ratifying a custom already in use. It is therefore possibly a practice dating from the time of the Apostles. This and the lavabo were doubtless derived from the Jewish ritual, where a similar rite is enjoined (*Exod.* xxx. 18) for Aaron and his sons.

115. In the English Church formerly, as still elsewhere, the priest after blessing the water before the Sunday morning service, went round and sprinkled the people with a bunch of hyssop while the choir sang "Purge me with hyssop, O Lord, and I shall be clean: wash me, and I shall be whiter than snow." Or in Eastertide, "I saw water coming forth of the temple out of the right side, Alleluia; and all upon whom this water came were saved and said Alleluia, Alleluia." This aspersion typified the dew of God's blessing which is shed upon those who worship Him aright.

116. Salt is mingled with the water so blessed, both in order to preserve it, and as a type of an incorrupt and innocent life.

117. The blessing and aspersion of water, although fallen into disuse in the English Church, are still legal, having never been formally abolished, and vessels for holy or blessed water having been permitted to remain in churches so late as the *sixth* year of Edward VI, four years subsequent to the year the ornaments in use in which are declared legal.

118. *Is not bread blessed in some parts of the Church?*

Yes; in the East; in France and elsewhere (as formerly in England) bread is blessed during Mass and distributed to the people as a token that they are in the Communion of the Church, even should they not communicate at that Mass, and also to take to sick persons for a like token.

119. *Why was the usage abrogated in England?*

Because it was thought the distribution of the blessed bread tended to make the common people neglect the reception of the sacrament.

120. *By what other names is the blessed bread known?*

In the East as the *eulogia* (i.e. the benediction, or token of good-will); in England it was called the "holy loaf."

121. *What ornaments of the Church and of the clergy are blessed?*

All those which from being directly used in connection with the Blessed Sacrament are called the *sacred* ornaments. These are the paten and chalice, the chalice veils, corporals, pall, and burse; the linen cloths of the altar: the chasuble, dalmatic, and tunic, with the stole and maniple. These after benediction should not be handled by lay people without permission. In addition to these, albs with their girdles, altar and processional crosses, and the like are blessed.

122. *Why do the canons specially require the above to be blessed prior to use, and forbid the laity to handle them without permission?*

Out of reverence to the Blessed Sacrament, in the celebration of which they are more immediately used. For the same reason in many parts of the Church they must be blessed by the bishop.

123. Corporals and other linen, which is brought into immediate contact with the Sacramental Presence, have for a similar reason to be washed by one in holy orders, prior to being washed by laics.

124. *Are any other things blessed for use in the Church service?*

The candles to be used in the Candlemas procession and the palms for Palm Sunday are blessed before use; and the paschal candle is blessed on Holy Saturday; incense is blessed prior to its use in the service; and also, as we have seen, the water about to be mingled in the chalice.

125. It is an ancient custom on Holy Saturday and Whitsun Eve to bless fire from which to kindle the lights. This signifies the spiritual joy with which we celebrate the Resurrection, and the Descent of the Holy Spirit in the likeness of fiery tongues. On the same days the font is blessed, because these two feasts were the chief days for conferring Baptism in the early Church.

126. *You have explained the use of blessed water; but why are things when blessed, generally sprinkled with it?*

Water is a symbol of God's blessing; the sprinkling therefore signifies that it is the dew of God's benediction, by the ministry of His priest, which consecrates material things to His service. It also shows that as by Baptism man, so through man the inanimate creation, is renewed and sanctified.

127. *What other benedictions are there?*

The most notable are the consecration of churches, altars, and churchyards or cemeteries; in addition to which the Church sanctions several benedictions, such as of a house, school, college, etc.; of fields and vineyards; of a newly-built ship; and the like.

128. *Why are churches consecrated?*

In order to set them apart for ever to the service of Almighty God, to separate them from profane uses, and to invoke the benediction of God upon, and His special presence within, the temple set apart to His worship.

129. *Why are altars consecrated?*

Because they are the more immediate seat of God's presence; His throne in the assembly of the faithful, and the place whereon the Holy Sacrifice is offered before God.

130. The portable slab of stone called the super-altar (see page 9, footnote), or the altar itself if made of stone, is anointed with holy oil when consecrated. Thus Jacob, when he took the stone which he had used for his pillow to make it an altar unto the Lord, poured oil upon it (*Gen.* xxviii. 18).

131. Oil is blessed for the purpose of anointing altars and super-altars; also for the anointing of the sick, according to the precept of S. James (chap. v. 14); for the anointing of the sovereign at his coronation, and in most parts of the Church for use at Baptism and Confirmation. In the Western Church, three kinds of oil are blessed by the bishop on Maundy Thursday. One, the *oil of the sick*, for the Sacrament of Unction; another, the *oil of catechumens*, for anointing candidates prior to Baptism; the third, a mixture of oil and balsam called the *chrism*, served for the anointing of altars, of the sovereign at his coronation, and for use at Baptism and Confirmation.[1]

132. *Why are churchyards and cemeteries consecrated?*

To be the last resting-places of the bodies of

---

[1] The oils so blessed are distributed to the parish priests of the diocese, for the anointing of the sick, of catechumens, and of newly baptized persons respectively; the anointing of altars, and confirmation of children, being confined to the bishop, and the anointing of sovereigns to the archbishop of the province. In the Eastern Church, however, the priest is allowed to confirm with chrism consecrated by the bishop.

the faithful; it being meet that the body made in Baptism the temple of the Holy Ghost (1 *Cor.* vi. 19); fed with the sacramental food of Christ's Body and Blood; sealed in Confirmation with the Holy Spirit; and hereafter to be raised (as the Church's hope for each one of her children is) in incorruption to immortal glory, should rest in hallowed ground.

133. The burial places reserved for those not in communion with the Church do not receive consecration, the Church's benedictions being only for her own children. When it is impossible from any cause to bury one in the Church's communion in consecrated ground the grave should be blessed previous to burial. A priest asked to bury the baptized child of Dissenting parents in Dissenters' ground would use this order, every baptized person being in the Church's communion, till by their own overt act of schism cut off from it.

134. *Are not persons blessed as well as places and things?*

Yes; the various benedictions occurring in the service are blessings of the congregation; so too the priest is directed to bless the newly married couple, the sick person when visited, etc.; and the bishop to bestow his blessing upon those he has confirmed or admitted to holy orders.

135. *Are there any other benedictions of persons?*

Yes; there is the setting apart of persons to any holy office or function in the Church of

God. When this setting apart is *sacramental* it is called *Ordination*, or in the case of bishops *Consecration*. Those not admitted to holy orders are set apart by a form of benediction. Of this kind are the forms of admission or benediction of choristers, acolytes, readers, the form of admission into a religious order, the institution of a religious superior, and the like.

136. The principle of Benedictions is carried out into the usages of domestic and social life. "Grace" before meals, or more properly the "Blessing of the Table," is an instance. This, as a solemn form of invoking God's blessing upon our food, should invariably be accompanied by the sign of the cross, not made, however, upon the food (the sign so made being a mark of *authority*, and as such being used in sacerdotal benedictions), but upon the person by the reciter and those present. The phrases "God bless you," "Good-bye" (that is, *God be with you*), "Adieu," and the like, are of a similar character.

SECTION V

FEASTS AND FASTS

137. *What are the great divisions of the Calendar?*

Every day is either a feast, a fast, or a feria; in addition to which the year is divided into certain seasons.

138. *Perhaps it will be simpler if you describe the seasons first.*

There are ten seasons: 1. *Advent*, which begins on the Sunday nearest the feast of S. Andrew (November 30th), and extends to Christmas Eve. 2. *Christmas*, which carries the year on to the Vigil of the Epiphany. 3. *Epiphany*, extending from January 6th to Septuagesima. 4. *Septuagesima*, from the Sunday of that name to Ash Wednesday. 5. *Lent*, extending to Easter Eve, and including 6, *Passiontide*, the fortnight before Easter. 7. *Eastertide*, from Easter Day to Whitsun Eve, in which is included 8, *Ascensiontide*, from the 5th Thursday after Easter to the Saturday week following. 9. *Whitsuntide*, being Whitsun Day and the six following days. 10. *The Trinity Season*, extending from Trinity Sunday to Advent.

139. *What do these seasons represent ?*

Advent commemorates the first and anticipates the second coming of our Lord; *Christmas*, His Birth; *Epiphany*, His manifestation to the Gentiles; *Septuagesima*, His labours and sorrows; *Lent*, His Fasting; *Passiontide*, His Suffering and Death; *Easter*, His Resurrection; *Ascensiontide*, His going up into heaven; *Whitsuntide*, the coming of the Holy Ghost; and *Trinity*, the final glory of the Elect in the fruition of the Beatific Vision.

140. *What is the respective length of these seasons ?*

Advent includes four Sundays; Christmas extends twelve days; the Sundays called "after Epiphany" vary from one to six, according as Easter falls early or late; Septuagesima includes the two next Sundays; Lent comprises six whole weeks from the Sunday after Ash Wednesday; Easter fifty days, ten of which, however, are counted in Ascensiontide; Whitsuntide seven days; the Sundays "after Trinity" vary from twenty-two to twenty-seven, from the same causes which regulate the number of those after Epiphany.

141. *Are there no other seasons ?*

The Ember days are called "the four Seasons;" or more properly "the fasts of the four Seasons," as occurring in the Spring, Summer, Autumn, and Winter quarters respectively.

They are the Wednesday, Friday, and Saturday after the first Sunday in Lent, Whitsun Day, the 14th of September, and the 13th of December.

142. *What are these fasts?*

Solemn seasons of prayer for the consecration of the four seasons; the bishops hold ordinations on the Sundays following these days.

143. *What other days are fasts?*

The forty days of Lent, the Rogation days, and the Vigils (or Eves) of Christmas, Easter, Ascension Day, Whitsun Day, the Purification and Annunciation of the Blessed Virgin Mary, SS. Matthias, John Baptist, Peter, James, Bartholomew, Matthew, Simon and Jude, Andrew, Thomas, and All Saints.

144. *What are the Rogation days?*

The Monday, Tuesday, and Wednesday before Ascension Day.

145. *Why are they so called?*

From the Latin word *rogare*, "to ask," because Litanies are then sung, *asking* for divers blessings, and especially for a benediction on the fruits of the earth.

146. *Why are the vigils of feasts observed as fasts?*

To prepare us for their proper observance in a spirit of sober joy; and as teaching us that we must *suffer* here in order to *rejoice* hereafter. They are symbolical of the sorrows of our Lord's earthly life, and of the probation which the saints underwent before they were fitted to reign with Christ.

147. Why, then, are the eves of certain feasts, as the Circumcision, the Epiphany, the Conversion of S. Paul, S. Mark, SS. Philip and James, S. Barnabas, S. Michael, S. Luke, S. Stephen, S. John, and the Holy Innocents, not observed as fasts?

All except S. Michael and S. Luke occur either in the Christmas or Easter seasons, when the Church is unwilling to multiply fasts. S. Michael's day is without a vigil, because the angels who are then commemorated did not undergo a state of probation on earth. S. Luke, not being one of "the twelve," his feast has not the distinction of being preceded by a vigil.

148. I see in the Prayer Book a "table of vigils, fasts, and days of abstinence." What is the distinction between these last?

Abstinence is a less strict observance than fasting. Fasting is the *total* abstinence from food up to a certain hour of the day (generally noon), and a diminution of *quantity* as well as *quality* in food. Abstinence is the mere refraining from animal food. Eggs, cheese, and butter are allowed in abstinence, but are forbidden in fasting.

FASTS AND FEASTS

149. *Are these days, then, to be observed as fasts or abstinence-days indiscriminately?*

Strictly speaking all the days set down in the table are *fasts* except the ordinary Fridays out of Lent, which are *days of abstinence*. But those who cannot fast should at least abstain on these days. Persons under age and in laborious work are not obliged to fast. Hence the distinction is not marked out with clearness.

150. *Why is Friday set apart as a day of abstinence?*

As a weekly memorial of our Lord's Passion; as Sunday is set apart as a weekly memorial of His Resurrection.

151. *What are feasts?*

Days set apart as solemn commemorations of our Lord, of the Blessed Virgin, of the Apostles; or of Martyrs, Virgins, Confessors, and other Saints.

152. *What are the Feasts that relate to our Lord?*

Christmas, the Circumcision, Epiphany, Easter, and Ascension Day; together with the Transfiguration (August 6), and the Name of Jesus (August 7). To these may be added Whitsun Day, the Feast of the Holy Trinity, and the Invention and Exaltation of the Cross.

153. *What Feasts relate to the Blessed Virgin?*

Those of her Purification (Feb. 2); Annunciation (March 25); Visitation (July 2); Assumption (Aug. 15); Nativity (Sept. 8); Conception (Dec. 8).

154. *Which are the Feasts of Apostles?*

SS. Andrew; Thomas; John; Conversion of S. Paul; Matthias; Mark; Philip and James; John *ante port. Lat.* (May 6); Barnabas; Peter; James; Lammas, or S. Peter's chains; Bartholomew; Matthew; Luke; Simon and Jude.

155. The other feasts are marked on the Calendar as those of "Martyrs," "Virgins," "Confessors," etc.

156. *Are all these feasts observed with equal importance?*

No; they are divided into several "classes."

157. *Why is this?*

So that if a movable feast clashes with a fixed one, or with an ordinary Sunday, the feast of lesser dignity may give place.

158. *What are the chief divisions of feasts?*

Major or red-letter days, and minor or black-letter days; so called because in the calendar they were formerly marked in red and black ink respectively.

159. *Are not these Feasts sometimes distinguished as "double" and "simple" Feasts?*

Yes; because formerly the anthem which

was sung at the *Magnificat* and *Benedictus* was "doubled," that is, sung throughout before as well as after the canticles on the major festivals, the initial words only being sung before on the lesser feasts.

160. In addition to the present red-letter days, the following were formerly "double feasts" in England: Wednesday in Easter and Whitsun week; Corpus Christi; Invention of the Cross (May 3); SS. Gregory (March 12); Ambrose (April 4); George (April 23); Augustine, Archbishop of Canterbury (May 26); Visitation of the Blessed Virgin (July 2); Transfiguration of our Lord (Aug. 6); Holy Name of Jesus (Aug. 7); Assumption of our Lady (Aug. 15); S. Augustine, bishop and doctor (Aug. 28); Nativity of the Blessed Virgin (Sept. 8); Exaltation of the Cross (Sept. 14); S. Jerome (Sept. 30); Translation of S. Edward the Confessor (Oct. 13); and the Conception of the Blessed Virgin (Dec. 8).

161. *If a major and a minor feast fall on the same day, the minor feast gives place. What happens if two major or two minor feasts fall on the same day?*

Each are subdivided into three or four classes, so that the feast of lower dignity still gives place.

162. *Are these classifications of any other use?*

Yes; they regulate the degree of dignity with which the service is to be performed.

163. *How so?*

On major feasts there are four rulers of the

choir by whom the *Venite* is sung on the feasts of the highest class; on the lower class major feasts it is sung by three of them. On minor feasts of the highest class there are three rulers; on those of the next class, two rulers; while simple feasts of the lowest class have no rulers.[1]

164. *Is there any other distinction?*

Yes; minor feasts of the lowest class have only one Evensong, while all the rest have two; added to which minor feasts of the two lower classes are never "translated." (See par. 171.)

165. *What do you mean by a feast having two Evensongs?*

I mean that its observance begins with the Evensong of the evening before. This is called its "first Vespers." The evening service of the day itself is the "second Vespers."

166. *Why is this observed?*

The Jews were wont to begin and end their Sabbaths and other feasts at sunset, in which custom the Christians followed them, but keeping them up to the midnight of the day itself, as a sign of the eternal rest (represented by the evening), in which they hoped to celebrate the true Sabbath that has no ending.

---

[1] Hence these days are known respectively as having quadruple, triple, double, or simple invitatory, and as being celebrated *cum*, or *sine*, *regimine chori*, with or without choir-rulers.

167. Mystically, the solemn commencement of a feast before the vigil fast had expired, or before the actual day of its observance had come, was held to represent the Divine Consolations with which the Saints were visited here in their state of probation; as an earnest that penitence is not without joy; and to remind us of the promises that "in due season we shall reap if we faint not;" "at eventide there shall be light."[1]

168. *How do feasts clash?*

In two ways: by "occurrence" and by "concurrence."

169. *When do feasts "occur"?*

When two or more fall on the same day.

170. *When do they "concur"?*

When they fall on two consecutive days, so that the second Evensong of the one is also the first Evensong of the other.

171. *What is done on such occasions?*

The greater feast is observed, sometimes with a commemoration of the lesser; at other times the lesser is "translated," i.e. transferred to the first vacant day.

172. *How is the lesser commemorated?*

Sometimes by its collect being said after that of the greater; sometimes by the use of its proper hymn at the end of the service, or in both ways.

---

[1] The first Vespers of Sunday has left a trace in the Saturday half-holiday still universally observed in schools, all work having formally ceased in time for the people to attend Evensong on Saturday.

173. *Are all Sundays of equal rank?*

Easter, Low, Whitsun, and Trinity Sunday are "double" feasts; of the rest, Advent Sunday, the first and fifth in Lent, and Palm Sunday, are called "Sundays of the first class;" the remaining Sundays in Advent and Lent, together with Septuagesima and the two following Sundays, are "Sundays of the second class."

174. *What is the rule when Sundays and festivals clash?*

Sundays of the first class take precedence of *all* feasts; Sundays of the second class of all but the highest. Ordinary Sundays yield to "double" feasts and simples of the highest class, but take precedence of others.

175. *What are octaves?*

Certain feasts are kept up for eight days; the eighth day is the octave-day, the intermediate days the days within the octave.

176. Octaves are observed to add greater dignity to the festivals. Thus Easter has been observed with an octave from the earliest times. Also (as Durandus says), as significant of the future glory of the Saint whose day is being observed, the day itself commemorating the event (as Christmas, our Lord's Birth), the octave day its future consummation, when we shall reap the full fruition. Sometimes the octave commemorates a distinct event, as the Octave of Christmas is observed as the feast of our Lord's Circumcision, wherein He *completed* His humiliation by taking upon Him the yoke of the Law;—the

FEASTS AND FASTS 51

Octave of Whitsun Day as Trinity Sunday, because the *end* of the Holy Spirit's outpouring on the Church is to lead us to the Beatific Vision of the Eternal Three in One.[1] Sometimes a feast has an octave, not only because of its dignity, but because of the many mysteries celebrated thereon. Thus, Epiphany commemorates not only our Lord's Manifestation, but also His Baptism and His first miracle at the Marriage of Cana.

177. *What rank have octave days and days within the octave?*

Some are observed as simples with rulers, and some as simples without.

In the modern Roman rite the octave day is a "double" of the lowest rank; the days within the octave are "semi-double," a description of feast answering to the simple with double invitatory of the English rites, and ranking with ordinary Sundays.

178. *What is a feria?*

A day which is not a feast.

179. *How are ferias distinguished?*

As ordinary and greater ferias.

180. *What are the greater ferias?*

The ferial days in Advent and Lent.

---

[1] The long and varying weeks "after Trinity" would thus express the *eternity* of the Beatific Vision; but this beautiful symbolism is peculiar to those Rites which number the Sundays in summer "after Trinity." When numbered after Whitsun Day, the Sundays thence to Advent are called "after Pentecost," and then the season is explained as representing the continual outpouring of the Holy Spirit upon the Church till the end of time.

181. *What is there to notice about them?*

They take precedence of certain kinds of feasts, which are only commemorated at these times.

182. Ash Wednesday, Maundy Thursday, and Good Friday, together with Easter and Whitsun Eves, are *principal ferias*, taking precedence of all feasts; the other days in Passion and Holy weeks take precedence of all minor feasts; the remaining weekdays in Lent, the Rogation days, and the weekdays in Advent, always take precedence of all minor feasts except those of the highest class. There is always a memorial or commemoration of the feria when a festival service is said on any of these days.

183. *What rank do vigils occupy?*

Vigils (with which rank Ember days) take precedence of simple feasts of the lowest class.

184. *What are the feasts of the Patron (or title) and of the Dedication of the church?*

The feast of the saint (or mystery) in whose honour the church was erected, and the anniversary of its consecration.

185. *How are these days observed?*

As major feasts of the first class (with an octave, except in Lent); and take precedence of all other feasts except Sundays of the first class, and the greater feasts of our Lord, the Vigils of Christmas and Pentecost, the Circumcision, Octave of the Epiphany, Ash Wednesday, Holy Week, Easter and Whitsun weeks, Ascension day, and All Saints' day.

SECTION VI

MATINS AND EVENSONG

186. *Why is the morning service of the Church called Matins?*

From the Latin *matutina*, which means "appertaining to the morning." From a similar cause the evening service is styled "Evensong."

187. *What is the object of these services?*

The constant singing of God's praises by means of the Psalter, which is sung through in regular course once a month, and the orderly reading of the Bible; in combination with which are offered acts of prayer for the needs of the worshippers, and of intercession for others.

188. *Why are these services directed to be sung "daily"?*

Because they represent the worship of the heavenly courts, which is continual.

189. *Why is the priest directed to say them "either privately or openly"?*

Because as a priest he is specially bound to praise God continually, a duty which he must not omit because the people neglect to join him in it; and because he is bound to offer the Church's intercession for all his flock, whether they themselves unite with him in bodily presence or not.

190. *What service of the Jewish Church do these offices represent?*

The "Service of Song" (1 *Chron.* vi. 31).

191. *Ought they then to be sung?*

Yes, wherever possible. Music is the fitting adjunct to the praises of God.

192. *I observe that the choir are ranged laterally in the chancel; and that they sing from side to side. Why is this?*

This mode of singing, which is called the "antiphonal," is of the greatest antiquity; so much so that it is said to have been instituted by S. Polycarp, the disciple of S. John, who saw in a vision the choirs of heaven chanting the praises of God in this manner.[1]

193. *I believe you call these two sides "Decani" and "Cantoris." For what reason?*

In cathedral churches the stall of the Dean (*Decani*) was to the right on entering the choir;

---

[1] Socrates, *Eccl. Hist.* The *Myrrour of Our Lady* gives a further reason: "The Psalms are sung sometimes on the one side and sometimes on the other, in token that the gifts of the Holy Ghost, whereby men do good deeds, are given some to one, some to another. But in singing of Psalms the choir standeth turned toward each other, and singeth face to face, in token that the gifts of God which each one hath received ought to be used to the helping each of other."

hence the south or Epistle side was called the side of the Dean ("Decani"). Opposite to him was the stall of the Precentor (*Cantoris*); and the north or Gospel side was called of the Precentor ("Cantoris").

194. *Why does the priest begin the more direct*[1] *portion of the service by the verse:* "*O Lord, open Thou our lips*"?

Because we cannot sing the praises of God without His assistance. For which cause it is a pious custom at this place to sign the lips with the sign of the cross, as the forehead and breast are signed at the next verse: "O God, make speed," etc.[2]

195. *Why does the "Gloria Patri" follow here?*

In token of our faith that God has heard us, and has opened our lips to sing His praise.

---

[1] In the first Prayer Book of Edward VI the Choir service began with the Lord's Prayer; and Bishop Cosin, who was principally concerned in the last revision, wished to make a marked separation between the respective portions of the service that preceded and followed the Lord's Prayer. In some MS. "directions to the printer" in his handwriting, he inserted after the Absolution: "Here set a fleuron," and on the next page before the Lord's Prayer: "Here set a fair compartment." In the first series of his notes on the Prayer Book (Works, v. 47) he wrote: "Here begins the service; for that which goes before is but a preparation to it; and is newly added in K. Edward VI's second book in imitation of the Liturgy and Mass of the Church of Rome. But as their Hours began with the Lord's Prayer, so begins our Matins, and the high service of the Altar."

[2] On the sign of the Cross, see paragraphs 243, 244, and the note subjoined.

196. *I observe that here and elsewhere, when this verse is sung, all in choir turn towards the East, and incline the head. Explain this.*

It is a solemn act of adoration to the Holy Trinity, whose praises are especially set forth in this doxology. For the same reason the people incline their heads at the first clause.

197. It is customary to *bow the head* at the Name of Jesus *whenever* it occurs in Divine service, and at any inscription of holiness to the Name of the Lord, as in the fourth verse of the *Magnificat*, Psalm cxi. 9, etc.), in veneration of that Name which "is as ointment poured forth," and in accordance with the express testimony of S. Paul (*Phil.* ii. 10), that "at the Name of Jesus every knee should bow."

198. On similar grounds the custom obtains of *bowing towards the Altar* on entering and leaving church, and whenever at other times passing in front of it. "Ye shall reverence My sanctuary," was God's command to the Jews, and the Christian sanctuary is holier than was the Jewish. It is moreover the expression by outward gesture of that exhortation of the Psalmist, "Fall down before *His footstool*, for He is holy." When the Blessed Sacrament is on the Altar, the custom is to *genuflect*, or *bow the knee*; and to this S. Augustine beautifully refers this very passage of the Psalmist (*Comment. on Ps. xcix*): "'Fall down before His footstool, for He is holy.' The Scripture says: 'The earth is the footstool of My feet.' I turn me to Christ, and I find Him here" (i.e. under the sacramental veils). "He took Earth of earth: for flesh is of earth, and of Mary He took Flesh. And since He walked here in this very Flesh, He hath given us this very Flesh to eat for our salvation" (i.e. in the Sacrament). "No one eats that Flesh except he first adore. We find therefore how we may adore the footstool of the Lord, and not only do we not sin in wor-

shipping, *but we sin if we worship not."* So our own Bishop Forbes says: " Christ in the Eucharist is to be adored with Divine worship, inasmuch as His living and glorified Body is present therein." Perfectly analogous, though of course infinitely lower in degree, is the ritual that obtains in civil life. Reverence is made before the throne of the sovereign, though he be not there; when he is there, men kneel, and kiss his extended hand.

199. *What is the " Venite " ?*

It is an introduction to the psalmody which now commences; for which reason it is called "the Invitatory Psalm."

200. *In singing the Psalms and Canticles, why does the cantoris side of the choir lead?*

Because that is the side of the precentor, whose office it is to lead the singing; and out of reverence to the Holy Gospel, which is read from this side of the altar.

201. *Why are the Glorias sung " full," i.e. by both sides of the choir ?*

Because the praises of the Blessed Trinity should be celebrated by every creature. Besides which, while the Psalms, being composed of prayer and confessions of sins as well as of praise, are fitly sung by the Church Militant, the ascription of blessing and glory to the Holy Trinity is sung alike by the Church Militant and the Church Triumphant.

202. *Why has the choir rulers ?*

To preside over the singing of the Psalms, that all may be done reverently and in order.

203. Are there always rulers of the choir?

No; only on major feasts, and minors of the two highest classes. At other times, the choir is presided over by the precentor.

204. Why do the rulers vary in number?

To mark the dignity of the feast. There are four on major feasts, two on minors.

205. Why do the rulers wear copes, and why do they sit during the Psalms, while the rest of the choir is standing?

They wear copes in honour of the "work of God" which is then being carried on; and as symbolical of the rule they possess over the choir; for which reason they sit, as also to be more at leisure to superintend the ritual of the Psalmody.

206. Why do they go to the lectern in turns before each Psalm?

To give out the "intonation, that is, the commencement of the Psalm, which the choir then take up. This is done alternately on the same principle as that on which the Psalms are sung from side to side.

207. Did the Church always surround the Psalms with ceremonial observances?

Yes; it was the custom in very early times to light lamps at the singing of the Psalms, as a sign of the joy and fervour with which we should celebrate the praises of God.

208. Formerly (and still in Religious Houses) the

Psalter was arranged so as to be sung through *every week*, by means of seven daily services, called the "Hours," in accordance with the words of the Psalmist, "Seven times a day do I praise Thee because of Thy righteous judgements" (*Ps.* cxix. 164), and the Night Office, or *Nocturns*, according to the saying of the same Psalmist, "At midnight I will rise to give thanks unto Thee" (*v.* 62). "I have thought upon Thy Name, O Lord, in the night-season" (*v.* 55). These "Hours" are described fully in the fifteenth section. In secular use the lesser hours came to be either altogether neglected or to be said by "accumulation"; that is, three or four services said continuously; and therefore when the Church arranged a vernacular Service-book, two daily choir-services were alone appointed, Matins, composed out of Matins, Lauds, and Prime; and Evensong, arranged from Evensong and Compline. The alteration necessarily involved a less frequent repetition of the Psalter. At the same time, the old canonical hours of prayer were recognized and provided for in private recitation in the various editions of the "Primer"; and would in all probability have been continued for monastic use had not the monasteries been suppressed before the reformation of the Service-books.

209. *What are the "tones" employed in the Psalter?*

They are the Gregorian scales modified into a melody, characterized by a *final* or tonic, and a *dominant* or reciting note. Fourteen such "Modes" are employed in the hymns and anthems of the Church, each of the seven scales admitting of two modes, having the same *final*, but a different *dominant*.[1] Of these "modes"

---

[1] The Gregorian dominant differs from the modern, which is invariably the fifth above the key-note.

the first eight only were employed in the Psalms and Canticles, each mode having its fixed melody. These melodies form the eight Gregorian "tones." A ninth called the "Eighth Irregular" or *tonus peregrinus*—the "foreign tone"—is added; its irregularity consisting in the two halves of the tone having a different dominant.

210. *Are these Tones employed in any recognised order?*

The first tone is styled "grave;" the second, "mournful;" the third, "exultant;" the fourth, "harmonious;" the fifth, "gladsome;" the sixth, "devout;" the seventh "angelical;" and the eighth, "sweet." They are generally distributed according to the character of the Psalms to which they are sung, or to the season.

211. The "Ambrosian" and "Parisian" tones are similar modifications of the Gregorian scales used respectively at Milan Cathedral and in some of the French churches.

212. *I see that the Psalter is "pointed" for singing. In what does this "pointing" consist?*

Each verse is marked off into two clauses by the colon (:), which corresponds to a similar division in the tones.

213. *Have not the tones more than two divisions?*

Ordinarily not. There are two changes from

the dominant, one in the middle, called the *meditation*, and one at the end, called the *cadence* or *ending*, each consisting of from one to five syllables. But on certain occasions a third division, called the *intonation*, appears.

214. *In what does the " intonation " consist ?*

In the prefixing of two or more notes to the dominant of the first clause.

215. *When is it used ?*

In the first verse of each Psalm, and of each verse of the *Gloria Patri* on festivals; in the ferial service at the beginning of the first Psalm only; and in penitential seasons not at all in the Psalter. In the canticles *Benedictus* and *Magnificat* it is used rather more frequently: always at the initial verse; and in the ferial service (not penitential) at both verses of the *Gloria Patri*; on festivals it is prefixed to every verse of these canticles.[1]

216. *Why is the intonation thus employed ?*

It is a festal feature in the " tones," and is

---

[1] The best authorities, however, say that the Evangelical Canticles should *always* be sung *festally*, i.e. with the intonation to every verse. And this would seem to have been the custom in the mediaeval Church of England. For in a MS. Breviary of Sarum use with the musical notation, preserved in the British Museum (Arundel MSS. 130), dated 1445, the eight tones for the *Benedictus* are thus prefaced, "*Benedictus*" (and of course equally *Magnificat*) "on account of its Evangelical authority, has this more beautiful mode in the intonation of psalmody and in jubilation." Chambers' Sar. Psal., p. 71 The Tones follow in *festal* form.

therefore more or less frequently used according to the solemnity of the occasion. It is sung at the *Gloria* because of the festal character of this Doxology, and to add solemnity to the praise of the Holy Trinity which is therein celebrated.

217. *What is the "pneuma" or slur?*

It consists of a few notes, either sung to the concluding syllable of the Psalms, or played on the organ.

218. *When is it used?*

At the end of the Psalm for the day, and at the end of the canticles *Benedictus* and *Magnificat* in the choir service, and of the *Te Deum* on festivals; and at the end of the sequence in the Holy Eucharist.

219. *Why are the Psalms finished with a pneuma?*

As a sign of our reluctance to quit the praises of God even for instruction and prayer.

220. *Is this custom old?*

The addition of a cadence to the "Alleluia" in the Eucharist, and to certain hymns when sung as sequences, is of some antiquity. Its use in this particular place is prescribed in the Old English Service-books, and was probably observed here from the time of St. Augustine.

MATINS AND EVENSONG 63

221. *Was the pneuma invariably used?*

No; it was omitted in Passiontide, when all marks of rejoicing are suppressed; in Easter-week, when the whole office was regarded as one continued act of praise; and in the Service for the Dead, in which the character of the psalmody was rather that of supplication than of praise.

222. A trace of the *pneuma* after the Psalms may be found in the "Voluntary," which in some churches is here introduced; only the *pneuma*, which, in accordance with the severe and chaste character of plain song, consisted of a few notes, winding out of the *Amen* as it were, and ending on the final of the mode in which the Psalms had been chanted, was replaced by a longer and more florid "performance," in which, as is generally the case in "Anglican" or Cathedral music, the symbolical meaning was sacrificed in order to give room to the *display* of the organist.

223. *Why are the Lessons read from a lectern?*

It is fitting that each ministration should have its proper place and appropriate furniture, that all things may be done decently and in order, and to the edifying of the flock. The lectern is therefore placed where the reader may be seen and heard of the people, in whose ears he is delivering the message of God, whether in the midst of the choir, or outside the screen.

224. In some cases the first lesson is read facing south, the second facing north; for the same reason

for which the Epistle and Gospel are recited respectively at the south and north corners of the altar, to signify the change from the Law of Moses to the Gospel of Christ. In reading the Old Testament, he slightly turns towards the altar, to signify that the prophecies were but indistinctly understood before the advent of Christ. The people heard the voice, as on Mount Sinai, but did not see the face of him that spake. In reading the New Testament, he slightly turns towards the people, to show that the Gospel of Christ and the Apostolic doctrine is not hid, but is preached everywhere.[1]

225. Another old custom is for the reader to beg the officiant's benediction before executing his ministry, which the latter bestows sitting. Bona, in speaking of a similar act of the deacon before reading the Gospel, thus explains the observance: "Before reading, he seeks from the celebrant a benediction, that is to say, license to read; for, as says Rupertus Abbas (lib. i. c. 12): 'None without mission or permission may assume the office of preaching; for how shall they preach except they be sent?'" The reader, therefore, like the seventy, goes forth to the people in the name and with the authority of the priest, as well as with his blessing for the due and reverent performance of his work.

226. *Why do the congregation sit during the Lessons?*

Because it is the general attitude of those who are being instructed. Also to avoid weariness, and in order to gather the mind,

---

[1] Mystical writers explain the reading of the Gospel (and similarly of our second Lesson) toward the *north*, as representing the putting to flight of Satan by the "glad tidings of salvation"—that Satan who said, "I will sit upon the mount of the congregation, in the sides of the north" (*Isa.* xiv. 13).

restfully to contemplate the mysteries revealed to us in Holy Scripture.

227. "The changing that is in God's service, from one thing to another," says the *Myrroure*, "is ordained to drive away your dullness, that ye should not wax tedious and weary, but gladly and joyfully—not in vain joy, but in joy of spiritual devotion—continue in God's service. Therefore sometime ye sing, sometime ye read, sometime ye hear; sometime ye sit, sometime ye stand, sometime ye incline, sometime ye kneel." "The Lessons are heard sitting, for knowledge of truth and right ruling of the will may not be but in a restful soul."

228. We *stand* at the Gospel in the Holy Eucharist, because it is there used liturgically, for which reason it can only be read in that place by one at the least in deacon's orders. Laymen may read the Lessons in the Choir service.[1]

229. *Why is the* Te Deum *sometimes omitted?*

It is considered a joyful and triumphant hymn, and is not, therefore, used in penitential seasons?

230. *Which are these seasons?*

Advent, and the season between Septuagesima and Easter, vigils, and three out of the four ember weeks.

231. *Why not all the ember weeks?*

Because one occurs in the octave of Pentecost,

---

[1] "After the commencement of the third antiphon let one of the boys in the dress of a reader bring the book of lessons to the proper place, who himself may read the lesson."—*Consuet. Sarum.*

during which solemnity it is not fitting that the *Te Deum* should be disused.

232. *Why is* Gloria Patri *not said at the end of the* Te Deum?

Because the whole hymn is a song of praise to the Holy Trinity. The Doxology would therefore be superfluous.

233. *I notice that the choir incline towards the altar at certain verses of this hymn. Why is this?*

At the verse "Holy, Holy, Holy," etc., for the same reason as at the *Gloria*; at the verse "When Thou tookest upon Thee to deliver man," in reverence to our Lord's Incarnation; at the verse, "We therefore pray Thee," both because praise at this verse is exchanged for prayer, and in veneration of our LORD'S Passion, which is spoken of at the end of the verse;[1] and at the verse, "O Lord, in Thee have I trusted,"[2] as expressing our trust in God, whose throne is represented by the altar, according to the words of the Psalmist, "I will lift up mine eyes unto the hills, from whence cometh my help." (*Ps.* cxxi. 1.)

234. *Why is incense used at the* Benedictus *and* Magnificat *when the service is solemnly performed?*

In honour of the Incarnation, which is espe-

---

[1] *Myrroure*, lxiv, lxv.   [2] *Consuet. Sarum*, 7.

cially celebrated in these, the "Evangelical" Canticles.

235. It was doubtless the ancient custom to offer incense *daily*, at least where sufficient was offered among the oblations of the people. The twofold offering of incense morning and evening thus answered to the "perpetual incense" of the Tabernacle (*Exod*. xxx. 7, 8), whilst its use in connection with the Holy Eucharist was a fulfilment of the prophecy that "in every place incense" should be "offered to the Name of the Lord, and a pure offering," or sacrifice (*Mal*. i. 11). In process of time the services came to be performed with less ceremonial on ferial than on Sundays and festal days, and so the offering of incense to be confined to the latter.[1]

236. *What are the ceremonies connected with it?*

The taper-bearers and thurifer, towards the close of the lesson, retire into the vestry, the former to light their tapers, the latter to prepare the incense. At its conclusion they return, and accompany the priest to the altar. He then puts incense into the censer, and with it censes the altar, first on the middle, then on the right side, then on the left, and again from left to right, where he gives the censer to the thurifer, who, with the taper-bearers, precedes

---

[1] The position which Matins has come to hold with us as a preparation merely for the High Celebration on Sundays and Festivals, has led to its being seldom "solemnly" performed. Hence the use of incense at the *Benedictus* is comparatively rare. Indeed it is obviously unwise to employ ritual to exalt the former, while so many of the non-communicants make assistance at the choir-service their whole Sunday worship.

him to his stall, where he censes him with three motions of the censer; next he censes the clergy in order, first those on the decani side, then those on the cantoris, using two motions of the censer; next the choir on either side in like manner; and, lastly, the congregation. Then, preceded by the taper-bearer, he carries the thurible back to the vestry.

237. Will you explain these incensations of the altar and choir?

The altar represents Christ, and by the incense with which the priest surrounds it, he signifies the truth of Christ's divinity, the solemn oblation of incense being an act of worship due to God alone (*Exod.* xxx. 37). It is also typical of the mercy-seat, and the cloud of incense which surrounds it symbolizes the intercessions which, in union with that of our Great High Priest, surround the throne of God on every side. The altar is censed in the midst first because that is the place of honour, being the spot where the Blessed Sacrament is consecrated;[1] afterwards on the Epistle side first, because to the Jewish Church first the ministry of intercession was committed to the

---

[1] After the priest has censed the Cross with three motions of the censer, he censes the upper part or retable first twice toward the Gospel side; then twice toward the Epistle side; then he censes the Altar itself first on the Epistle side, as described above. This signifies that the Gospel existed in the purpose of God before all time, and was therefore really anterior to the Law.

Christian Church; then again from the Gospel to the Epistle side, in token that Jew and Gentile are all one in Christ. The congregation are censed in acknowledgement that through the Incarnation all are partakers of the Divine Nature: and in order, first the clergy, next the choir, lastly the laity, to show that, though all one in Christ, all members have not the like honour. But whereas men are only in a certain sense partakers of the Divine Nature, which is directly allied to the human alone in Christ; therefore the priest alone censes the altar, while the choir and people are censed by an inferior minister.[1]

238. *What should be our thoughts at the offering of the incense?*

We should earnestly desire that our prayers might ascend as the incense in God's sight, and that by our holiness of life we may offer ourselves to Him in the odour of sweetness. We may offer Him the precious merits of Christ's Life and Passion—which is, indeed, a sacrifice of a sweet-smelling savour in His sight, and which is being specially pleaded at the time of incense, whether at the Evangelical Canticles, or in the Eucharistic sacrifice. And when the

---

[1] Cardinal Bona gives as the symbolic teaching of the censing of the people the spirit of prayer, and the grace of God that is shed abroad in our hearts. "The incensing of the ministers and of the laity around is performed as pertaining to religion; namely, with the intent to stir up to prayer and to represent the effect of Divine grace."

minister brings the censer towards us we should pray that, by the grace of God shed abroad in our hearts, those merits may be communicated to us individually, and to those for whom we are more especially bound to pray.

239. The Canticles *Benedictus* and *Magnificat* have ever been regarded as invariable *Gospels*, sung Psalm-fashion. Thus the *Myrroure*—"Ye have in your service three Gospels, that is, *Benedictus* and *Magnificat* and *Nunc Dimittis*:[1] and all three are sung standing for reverence of the Gospel" (*Myr.* lxx). Hence lights and incense were used here as in the Gospel. With regard to the use of lights in connection with the Gospel, we have the express testimony of S. Jerome to its antiquity. "Throughout all the Churches of the East," he says, "when the Gospel is about to be read, tapers are lighted, though it be broad daylight, not to scatter the darkness, but as a sign of joy . . . that under the symbol of bodily light, that light may be shadowed forth of which we read in the Psalter, 'Thy word, O Lord, is a lantern unto my feet, and a light unto my paths'" (*Epist adv. Vigilant*). The Jews have a similar observance in their synagogues at the reading of the Law, and probably for similar reasons.

240. *Why do we stand at the Creed?*

To show that faith without works is dead; that what we believe in our heart we must not only declare with our lips, but show forth in our lives. It is sung towards the east, because such was the attitude used in all the more solemn parts of the service, and as signifying that a

---

[1] Incense, however, was not burned at *Nunc Dimittis*, because it belonged to Compline, which as one of the lesser hours was never sung "solemnly."

right faith, like every other good and perfect gift, cometh down from the Father of lights, and must be sought from Him by diligent prayer.

241. *Why are the two last clauses of the Creed and of the Lord's Prayer sung with inflexions like the versicles?*

Anciently, when the "discipline of the secret" prevailed, the catechumens were not taught the Creed and the Lord's Prayer till just before Baptism. Hence these were never said aloud except in the Mass, when no unbaptized persons were supposed to be present. This custom was retained after its cause had ceased, and the priest and choir chanted the last two clauses as a signal that the Creed or Lord's Prayer was finished.

242. S. Benedict first introduced the custom of saying the Lord's Prayer *aloud* at Lauds and Vespers; and from him the usage became general in the West. At the other hours it is still said secretly.

The *Myrroure* assigns a mystical reason for the usage. According to it the Apostles' Creed was recited privately because it was made before the Gospel was openly preached, while the Nicene and Athanasian Creeds, which were afterwards written against certain heresies, were said aloud, "to the strength of our faith and confusion of heretics."

243. *I perceive that many persons make the sign of the Cross at the end of the Creed and the Lord's Prayer. Will you explain the reason?*

As to the use of the sign of the Cross in

general, I will reply in the words of the 30th canon of 1603. The bishops are speaking of the sign of the Cross in Baptism; but, as you will see, they bear witness to the antiquity of the custom of using it at other times: "The honour and dignity of the name of the Cross begat a reverend estimation even in the Apostles' times (for aught that is known to the contrary) of the sign of the Cross, which the Christians shortly after used in all their actions: thereby making an outward show and profession, even to the astonishment of the Jews, that they were not ashamed to acknowledge Him for their Lord and Saviour Who died for them upon the Cross." Similarly Bishop Montague: "If it be not superstitious to sign on the forehead, why is it to sign in any other part of the body? Why more out of Baptism than in Baptism? Is one part of the body more subject to superstition than another? What hindereth it but that I may sign myself with the sign of the Cross in any part of my body at any time, at night when I go to bed, in the morning when I rise? The ancient Church so used it out of Baptism, and so may we." Its use *here* appears to have arisen from the custom alluded to above, of beginning and ending (first the *day*—afterwards) any special action with the sign of the Cross. Thus the people were wont to sign themselves at the end of the more solemn parts of the service, as the Gospel (and for the same reason the three

"Evangelical" Canticles), Creed, Lord's Prayer, *Gloria in Excelsis, Sanctus,* etc., and when the priest bestows his benediction.[1]

244. The sign of the Cross is a short creed in action. First, it represents our belief in the Crucified, and our trust in His Passion. Next, it declares our faith in the Holy Trinity, to whom we have access by the Cross of Christ. For first we place our hand to our forehead, *in the Name of the Father,* Who is God over all; then to the bottom of the breast, *and of the Son,* Who humbled Himself even to the death of the Cross; and, lastly, from the left to the right side, *and of the Holy Ghost,* Who proceedeth both from Father and Son. Or, as the *Myrroure* explains it, by the sign of the Cross we express our belief that "our Lord Jesus Christ came down from *the Head,* that is the Father, unto earth by His Holy Incarnation; and then from the earth unto the *left side,* that is hell, by His bitter Passion; and from thence to His Father's *right side* by His glorious Ascension.

245. *What is the meaning of the verse " The Lord be with you," and its response ?*

It is a very ancient mode of salutation in the Christian Church, having been borrowed apparently from the Jews. (See *Ruth* ii. 4.) The priest, being now about to engage in prayer and intercession, turns towards the people, and extending his hands, salutes them as his brethren in Christ, in token that they are partakers with

---

[1] At the same time this custom, though ancient, is entirely optional, and is expressly left to each one's devotion. "As touching *crossing,* holding up of hands, knocking upon the breast, and other gestures, they may be used or left, as every man's devotion serveth" (*Edward VI's First Prayer Book,* "Certain Notes for the more plain explication," etc.).

him in the prayers that follow; and they reply similarly in acknowledgement that, though it belongs to him by virtue of his office to intercede for them, they on their part bear him up by their prayers.

246. *Why does he extend his hands?*

As a sign of charity, and in token of his anxious desire that they may be partakers of the grace for which he is about to pray.

247. *At the words "Let us pray" he joins his hands. Wherefore?*

To signify that the prayers of priest and people are, as it were, joined in one; that he is about to pray, not in his own name alone, but in the name of all present, or rather of the whole Church. For the same reason all sing together the *Kyrie eleison*, or "Lord, have mercy upon us," and all recite together the Lord's Prayer.

248. *Why does the priest stand up at the Versicles and Collect?*

Because he offers these acts of intercession ministerially. For which cause, according to ancient custom, he should descend from his stall and stand in the midst of the choir, facing east, till after the last Collect.[1]

---

[1] The Sarum rubric is: "Let the priest stand up, and proceed to the step of the choir at Matins and Evensong, and there say these verses." The Collect was universally said standing; and it is difficult to conceive how the contrary custom crept in, as the "*all* kneeling" of our rubric

249. When the service is said by one not in priest's orders these versicles are said kneeling, because the officiant is not authorized to offer them ministerially.

250. *What is the "Anthem"?*

Any musical composition, whether metrical or prose, bearing upon the services of the day. The term was formerly applied to certain detached verses (more properly called "Antiphons") appended to the Psalms and Canticles. Anthems, in the Cathedral sense, are of extremly modern date, being introduced in the time of Queen Elizabeth to supply the loss of the Hymns which Archbishop Cranmer wished translated for the reformed services, but could not obtain. As these have since been translated it is usual to sing them here in place of the Anthem.

251. *How are these hymns arranged?*

In the ordinary service they commemorate the order of the creation, except that for Saturday at Evensong, which is a prayer to the Holy Trinity for light. The various seasons have

---

need not refer to the priest. From the *Myrroure* we learn that the Collect was said "turned toward the east, for Paradise, from whence we are expelled, is in the east, and therefore thinking what we have lost, and where we are, and whither we desire, we pray turned towards the east" (*Myr.* lxxii). ¶ A boy held the book for the priest to say the Collects *junctis manibus*, and in the solemn service the taper-bearers stood on either side of him facing each other. The lights symbolize the fervour with which our prayers should be made to God, and were also intended to mark the dignity of the Collect as the Eucharistic feature in the choir service.

proper hymns commemorating the mystery therein celebrated. Thus, the Advent, Christmas, Epiphany, Ascension, and Whitsun seasons have each Proper Office Hymns for Morning and Evening. So has Eastertide, with an additional one for Saturdays at Evensong. There are also Proper Hymns for Trinity Sunday, S. Stephen, Holy Innocents, the Invention and Exaltation of the Cross, S. John Baptist, S. Mary Magdalene, the Transfiguration and Holy Name of Jesus, S. Michael, and All Saints' Day; and for the feasts of Apostles and Evangelists in and out of Eastertide, of one and of many Martyrs, of Confessors, of Virgins, of Holy Women, and of the Blessed Virgin Mary.

252. *How are these hymns distinguished?*

The hymns throughout the week in the Epiphany and Trinity seasons are called the "Ordinary of the Season"; those for the other seasons are the "Proper of the Season." Similarly, the hymns common to all Saints of any class, as Martyrs, Virgins, etc., are the "Common of Saints"; those appointed especially for any saint form the "Proper of Saints."

253. *How are the hymns sung?*

To a proper plain-song melody, written in one of the fourteen Gregorian modes. They are begun by the precentor, or rulers of the choir, like the Psalms, and sung verse by verse on alternate sides, both choirs joining at the Dóxology, and facing eastward as at the *Gloria*. The pneuma is not used, unless the hymn be employed as a sequence.

254. *Are not hymns sung at other times except in place of the anthem?*

Yes; at the end of Matins and Evensong, when a "Memorial" has to be made; and if there is no memorial, at the discretion of the clergy; as also before and after the sermon, etc.

255. *What is a "Memorial?"*

It is the commemoration of a lesser feast which falls on the same day as a greater. The "Office" of the latter is said, and a "Memorial" made of the former. This is done (with us) by the use of its proper hymn at the end of the service.

256. The other hymns being of a less liturgical character, are generally sung with more freedom, to tunes composed in the modern scales, and by both sides of the choir.

NOTE.—Present-day students of the Sarum Rite would not perhaps allow Mr. Walker's description, in this section, of what mediaeval precedent would sanction (as the proper ceremonial to be observed when Matins and Evensong are solemnly chanted), to be exact in all respects; it gives, however, a fairly accurate account of the ceremonial which it deals with. [B.]

SECTION VII

SOLEMN TE DEUM

257. *Is not the* Te Deum *sometimes employed as a separate service?*

Yes; in times of general or particular thanksgiving. It usually, however, follows the Eucharist or Evensong on these occasions.

258. *What are the attendant ceremonies?*

The priest is vested in a white cope, that being the vestment appointed for all solemn functions beside the Eucharist, and white being the colour appropriate for rejoicing. He is attended by the taper-bearers and thurifer, the latter with smoking censer, though the incense is not "offered"—that is, the priest does not cense the altar, nor take the censer into his hands.

259. *Why is this?*

Incense is used here as a sign of rejoicing, but it is not offered, because the *Te Deum*, as a separate service, is not a liturgical office, apart from which the priest does not offer incense.

SECTION VIII

THE LITANY

260. *Why is the Litany recited at a desk outside the choir screen?*

Because it is a penitential service, and for such this is the most fitting place, as appears from that of Joel (ch. ii. 17): "Let the priests, the ministers of the Lord, weep *between the porch and the altar*, and let them say, Spare Thy people, O Lord." The priest also descends into the body of the church to show that, no less than the people, he has need to deplore his sins.

261. *Is the Litany ever "solemnly" sung?*

Yes; on the Rogation Days, and on Ash Wednesday. The officiant wears a cope,[1] and is assisted by the choir. On the former occasion it is sung in procession; but on Ash Wednesday at the usual place.

262. *Why is the Litany sung with greater solemnity at these times?*

In the former case to implore a blessing on the fruits of the earth; in the latter, as

---

[1] This is *red* according to Old English, *violet* according to Roman use.

an appropriate introduction to the Lenten fast.[1]

---

[1] The Litany is solemnly sung on the three last days of Holy Week and on the Vigil of Pentecost for a similar reason as on Ash Wednesday; and on the Feast of S. Mark to implore freedom from pestilence, S. Gregory the Great having put a stop to a plague in Rome by a solemn procession with litanies in A.D. 590; similarly in any time of public calamity.

NOTE.—I am unable to discover on what ceremonial code the directions or descriptions in these sections (VII, VIII) are based; they do not seem to be derived from the author's usual authorities. The altar certainly was censed during the *Te Deum* at Matins, according to some rites, and it is difficult to see the force of the reason given for not observing this ceremony in paragraph 259. I know of no ancient precedent for a solemn chanting of the Litany on Ash Wednesday, Maundy Thursday, or Good Friday. [B.]

SECTION IX

PROCESSIONS

263. *What are Processions?*

Hymns, Psalms, or Litanies chanted by the clergy and people *marching* in formal order. They are of two kinds, *festival* and *penitential.*

264. *Why are Processions used?*

Festival processions represent the progress of the Church, according to the prophecy of the Psalmist: "They will *go* from strength to strength." In *penitential* processions the idea is different. In these the Church, as it were, "goeth on her way weeping," yet bearing the good seed of supplication and prayer, and looking to come again with joy, bringing her sheaves with her (*Ps.* cxxvi. 7). In the one, the future *triumph* of the Church is depicted; in the other, her present *pilgrimage* through this vale of misery.

265. *Why are Processions headed by the Cross?*

As a token that through the Cross alone the Church can attain her triumph, or go safely in this her exile—that the Cross sanctifies alike her joy and her sorrow. The Cross going before serves also to show that alike in her triumph and in her trial she does but follow the steps of Christ crucified, Who in His earthly ministry was like His great Apostle "in journeyings oft" for the salvation of souls, till at length He "went up" to Jerusalem, and along the "way of sorrows" to the Mount of Calvary; and afterward, having risen glorious from the grave, "went up on high," and sat down at the right hand of God.

266. According to old English use the Processional Cross on all the Sundays in Lent, except the first, is of wood painted red and without the figure of our Lord, and in Eastertide till the Ascension of crystal or glass. The first points to the bloody Passion of our Lord, and His immolation on the wooden altar of the Cross; the second to the triumph and joy of that holy season in which our Lord's Body rose from the tomb, no longer liable to weakness and death, but impassible and glorious, and the cross from an ensign of shame became a standard of victory and rejoicing.

267. *Why are banners employed?*

Partly to kindle the devotion of the people, and partly for mystical reasons. Thus, in *festal* processions, to signify yet more clearly the progress and future triumph of the Church, according to that description of her in the Canticles (ch. vi. 10): "Who is she that looketh forth as the morning, fair as the moon, clear as the sun, and terrible as an army with banners?" So in *penitential* processions (though more sparingly) to show that in her pilgrimage here she is the Lord's host, drawn up in battle array; or to express her hope of deliverance, according to the words of the Psalmist, when he strove with the King of Zobah (2 *Sam.* viii. 3); "Thou hast showed Thy people hard things; Thou hast made us to drink the wine of astonishment. [Yet] Thou hast given a banner to them that fear Thee, that it may be displayed, because of the truth, that Thy beloved may be delivered" (*Ps.* lx. 3–5).

268. In the old English rite two banners, one bearing the device of a lion and the other of a dragon, were employed in the Rogation Processions and in that on Ascension Day. In the former the dragon went first in place of the cross, the lion coming behind; in the latter the lion went first, the dragon behind. This was to symbolize that the earth was cursed for man's sake and given over to the dominion of Satan, that great dragon (*Rev.* xii. 3); but that Christ, "the Lion of the tribe of Judah" (*Rev.* v. 5), by His Resurrection and Ascension, had rescued it from his dominion.

269. *In Processions the place of honour appears to be at the end, those of lowest rank going first, then those of higher grade in order, till the Bishop or principal dignitary closes the line. Will you explain this?*

The Church probably adopted the custom from the ceremonial employed in civil life; in which the sovereign was preceded by heralds and other functionaries, the place of honour of course being near the person of the sovereign.

270. It may interest the reader to remind him that the very first service performed in England by

S. Augustine and his band of missionaries was a Litany in Procession. They came, says Bede, "bearing a silver cross for their ensign, and the image of our Lord and Saviour painted on a board . . . and as they drew near to the city with the holy cross and the banner of our sovereign Lord and King Jesus Christ, they sang with one accord this Litany: 'Lord, we pray Thee of Thy mercy, take away Thine anger from this city, and from Thy holy house, for we have sinned. Alleluia.'"

271. *When are Processions employed?*

According to Western use there is a procession every Sunday and greater festival before solemn celebration. To this the old English uses add a procession after Evensong on feasts, and on, Saturday evenings from Easter to Advent. On *Candlemas Day* those in procession carry lighted tapers in allusion to the prophecy of Symeon, "A light to lighten the Gentiles"; and on *Palm Sunday* branches of palm in commemoration of our Lord's triumphal entry into Jerusalem, when the people took branches of palm and strewed them in the way. The Litany is sung in procession on the Rogation days, and on the Feast of S. Mark, as has been explained in the preceding section (see pars. 261, 262, and note).

Special processions, whether to beg blessings from God, or to render Him thanks, take place as occasion serves.

272. *Explain the proper order of Processions.*

The priest, with the taper-bearers, etc., goes to the midst of the chancel before the altar-steps, and there puts incense into the censer as at the *Magnificat*; the procession then starts from the Epistle side, and passing down the south aisle returns through the nave.

273. The old English use was to employ the inverse order in *penitential* processions, passing down the *north* aisle and returning by the nave. In cathedrals and larger churches, the procession on feast days and other solemn occasions quitted the choir by the north door of the presbytery, and passed behind the high altar, so reaching the south aisle and returning by the nave.

It is usual to sing a Hymn or Psalm in processions. The old Office-books or "Processionals" give an Antiphon or Anthem for every Sunday, to which is added, except from Palm to Trinity Sundays, a "Prose" with versicle, response, and Collect, to be sung "in the station," i.e. standing in the nave before the choir screen; and another Antiphon on entering the choir. On festivals a Hymn follows the first Antipon, or "Responsory," as it is called. Archbishop Cranmer wished to set forth the processions in English, but was prevented from carrying out his design,

SECTION X

LOW CELEBRATION

[Any ceremonies not explained in this section must be sought for in the next, on "High or Solemn Celebration."]

274. *What do you mean by Low Celebration?*

I mean the administration of the Holy Communion without the adjuncts of assistant ministers and choir. It is wont to be thus administered in the early mornings and on weekdays.

275. Originally the Holy Eucharist, as the chief service of the Church, was invariably offered with the *full ceremonial*, as it still is in the Greek Church; but as the number of communicants increased it was found necessary to multiply celebrations; and the number of clergy being insufficient for the "solemn" performance of all, the custom arose of "Low" or "simple" celebrations, with the priest and a server.

276. *Why is the priest attended by a server?*

Partly in honour of his office, partly to avoid the unseemly necessity of leaving the altar to take journeys backwards and forwards to the credence-table.

277. For the first of these reasons a bishop has *two* servers at a low celebration.

278. *What are the duties of the server?*

1. To make the responses; in which sense

he represents the choir, and thus as it were by his presence protests that it is only under stress of circumstances that the Church permits her highest act of worship to be solemnized without the aid of music. 2. To minister to the priest. This he does by bringing the bread and wine from the credence; by collecting or receiving the alms; by holding up the edge of the chasuble when the priest kneels; and by bringing the wine and water for the ablutions. In these functions he represents the "ministers," i.e. the deacon, subdeacon, and acolytes, at a High Celebration. He also assists the priest to vest and unvest in the vestry.

279. *How is the server vested ?*

Generally in cassock and surplice, or rather *rochet* (or cotta),[1] which differs from the surplice in having tight arms. These are more convenient for the server to minister in. Sometimes, however, when the service is said under peculiar circumstances, as when from any cause the chief Sunday service is a Low Celebration, the server wears the girded alb. See par. **66.**

280. The priest wears his Eucharistic vestments. See section iii, more especially paragraphs 75-90.

281. The server is generally a boy, the Church having from the earliest times consecrated *all ages* to the service of the sanctuary. Children were thus admitted to minister before the Lord, as was the child Samuel

---
[1] For a description of these vestments, see paragraphs 62, 63.

(2 *Sam.* ii. 11). They were formerly set apart for this service by Episcopal benediction. *Lectors* or "readers" were required to be above the age of infancy, i.e. seven years; *acolytes* (from the Greek ἀκόλουθος, an attendant, or minister), were admitted at the age of fourteen. It is usual to admit boys into a choir with a form of prayer and blessing; and to choose from among their number the steadiest and most devoutly disposed to act as servers and acolytes.

282. *This service is sometimes called Low "Mass," is it not; as the "solemn" celebration is called "High Mass"? Will you explain this term? Also the word "Eucharist," which I see frequently made use of?*

The only thing that seems to be certain about the term "Mass" is, that, originally, it had no special doctrinal signification. It appears first in the 4th century as an already recognized term for the celebration of the Eucharist. But it would seem to have been also used in subsequent times, at least occasionally, to designate other offices of public or common worship. It was, however, chiefly employed as a title of the Eucharist celebration. As to the original derivation of the word, scholars and antiquarians are at hopeless disagreement. No competent scholar will have anything to say to the pretended Hebrew origin of the term. A widely received opinion is, that as at the conclusion of the different stages of the Eucharistic service, the deacon gave the signal to those who were to depart with the words *Ite, missa est*, the word *missa* got to be taken by the vulgar in a mistaken sense. *Missa*, it is said, is low Latin for *missio = dismissio*, i.e. dismissal, but as used by the deacon it was thought to be the title of the service, and so " Depart, it is the dismissal," was imagined to mean " Depart, Mass is over." This is rather a lame explanation, but it is one that has found much favour. The simple fact is, that the philology of the word is lost in obscurity ; but for a thousand years and more the term has been used to signify the Eucharistic celebration, and was so used by our forefathers, till it was discredited by having a polemical meaning arbitrarily attached to it. It is time that good sense prevailed, and that the ancient and venerable term " Mass" was once more restored to its traditional place in our ecclesiastical nomenclature. Eastern Catholics, when they use a Western language, usually call their own Liturgy, " the Mass ; " the term may thus claim to have gained a place in the terminology of the " whole Catholic Church of Christ." [B.]

The term *Eucharist* is derived from the Greek, and signifies " thanksgiving."

283. The Greeks call the Eucharist the *Liturgy*, i.e. the public work or ministry, and also *Synaxis*—the "assembly." Both these words occur in the Scriptures, the former (*Acts* xiii. 2): "As they ministered to the Lord (i.e. said the liturgy, λειτουργούντων) and fasted;" and again (*Heb.* x. 11): "Every (Jewish) priest standeth daily ministering ('liturgizing'), and offering ofttimes the same sacrifices;" the latter (*Lev.* xxiii. 36): "Ye shall offer an offering made by fire unto the Lord: it is a solemn assembly."

284. *But does not the thirty-first Article condemn the Mass by that very name?*

A moment's reflection will serve to show that such is not the case. For by the Mass is simply meant the Sacrament of the Lord's Supper. A received Catholic opinion is that all that is *necessary* (though more may be *desirable* for solemnity's sake) for the celebration of the Mass, is that a lawful minister use the words and gestures of Christ over the appointed elements of bread and wine, of which he afterwards partakes. Now all these conditions are preserved in the Prayer Book as necessary to a valid administration of the Lord's Supper. Hence the Church could not condemn the Mass without condemning the institution of Christ. All that she could say would be that the Holy Eucharist, commonly called the Mass, was wrongly so called, because it was not a veritable sacrificial offering. But her best divines have ever taught the reverse. Thus Bishop Overall, who drew up the last part of the Catechism, says: " It is a plain Oblation of Christ's Death once offered, and a representative Sacrifice of it for the sins and for the benefit of the whole world." And Bishop Andrewes: " The Eucharist ever was, and by us is considered, both as a Sacrament and a Sacrifice." And again, Bishop Cosin, who was chiefly employed by the Church in the last revision of the Prayer Book: " We call the Eucharist a propitiatory Sacrifice, both this and that (i.e. the Sacrifice on Calvary), because both of them have force and virtue to appease God's wrath against this sinful world." The doctrine which the Article condemns is the doctrine that the Holy Eucharist is a sacrifice in such a sense as to interfere with the unity and completeness of the Sacrifice on Calvary —the great propitiatory freewill offering of Himself by Christ—that it is an *independent repetition*, not a continuation and renewed *application* of that Sacrifice.

285. The Latin Mass continued to be used under that name till 1549, "without the varying of any rite or ceremony," except that after the Communion of the priest he addressed certain exhortations to the communicants in the mother tongue, and then proceeded to communicate them in both kinds. In this form, however, it was said that "other order" (for " varying of [some] other rites and ceremonies in the Mass ") should " be provided." This was done in the summer of 1549, when Edward VI's First Prayer Book, containing " the Supper of the Lord and the Holy Communion, *commonly called the Mass*," came into force. It was, in fact, the Old Mass with the promised " varying " of certain " rites and ceremonies." In 1552 the Articles were first promulgated, and among them that now numbered XXXI. The same year the Second Prayer Book received the sanction of Parliament, which took occasion, however, to say that the changes (which included the omission of the term " Mass "), were occasioned " rather by the curiosity of the ministers and mistakers, than from any other WORTHY cause," as an Act two years before had done to declare that the First Book (which contained the term) had been drawn up " BY THE AID OF THE HOLY

GHOST." The Article, therefore, *could* not have been aimed against the term "Mass," nor against any doctrine necessarily involved in that term; since both had been sanctioned by the Liturgy which had just been declared the *true and unbiassed voice* of the English Church, assisted by the Spirit of truth.

The term lingered at least so late as 1561, under which date an entry exists: "Paid for 4 lbs. of candles on Christmas-day morning *for the Mass,* 12*d.*; and among the Puritans, the Order in the Prayer Book was ordinarily spoken of as 'the English Mass.'"

286. The priest enters carrying the sacred vessels under a veil. Why is this?

From motives of reverence; for which cause also he spreads the corporal or fine linen cloth on the altar, and then deposits the chalice (still veiled) on it. The veil is made of silk, and varies in colour, according to the season. See par. 34, 36, 101, 104.

287. Why does the priest begin the service at the side of the altar?

It was ever the custom to perform the preparatory and subordinate parts of the service at the side, reserving the midst of the altar for the more solemn portions. The service used to begin at the "Epistle" or south side, probably because of the introductory and subordinate character of the Epistle, as compared with the Gospel. Our own more general custom of beginning at the north or "Gospel" side appears to have arisen from the confusion between the rubrical directions in the two

Prayer Books of Edward VI, the first of which contemplated the old order remaining intact, while the second, in directing the altar to be placed table-wise (that is with one of its narrow ends towards the people), still placed the priest in the midst of what in the old arrangement was the front, but was now the "north side" of the altar. When the altars were brought back into their proper position, the rubric by an oversight remained unaltered. Many ritualists therefore hold that the present rubric has been virtually abolished by the successful attempt of Archbishop Laud to bring back the altars to their old position, and therefore begin the service according to ancient custom, at the "Epistle" side.

288. *I have noticed the priest, after having deposited the sacred vessels on the altar, descend and stand awhile in private prayer. Why does he do this?*

To prepare himself for the service in which he is about to engage. For the same reason he has already recited the hymn, "Come, Holy Ghost," or certain other prayers, in the vestry. Before the altar he usually says privately the Psalm, "Give sentence with me, O God" (*Ps.* xliii), the fitness of which you will readily see; then going to the altar, he may say, privately, the "Introit" for the day, adding aloud the Lord's Prayer and the Collect, "Almighty God, unto whom all hearts be open." In the former of these prayers the server makes no reply, because, though said aloud, it is part of the priest's preparation; to the latter he replies "Amen," extending the preparation to the people.

289. *Why does the priest now turn to the people?*

To read the Lesson from Exodus xx. It was an ancient custom, especially in penitential seasons, to read lessons from the Old Testament at the beginning of the Mass. The lesson here given is interspersed with responses, which consist of the ninefold "*Kyrie Eleison*," or, "Lord, have mercy upon us," said thrice to God the Father, thrice to God the Son, and thrice to God the Holy Ghost; to each Person, as an old treatise says, because we sin against each; and *thrice* to each, because we offend in three ways—in thought, word, and deed. After the Tenth Commandment, another and slightly varied *Kyrie* is said, corresponding to a prayer for remission of sins, which was wont to be here said.

290. *Why does the prayer for the sovereign follow here?*

In accordance with the command of S. Paul (1 *Tim.* ii. 2), that prayers and supplications should be made for kings and those in authority.

291. In both Prayer Books of Edward, and in those of Elizabeth, etc., the priest was directed, according to

the old order, to say first the Collect or Collects for the day, then one of the two for the king. The present inverse order is probably an oversight.

292. *Where the service has been hitherto said at the north side (see par. 287), I see that the server here removes the book to the Epistle corner, where the priest says the Collect. Why is this?*

Because we here begin a new stage of the service. What has gone before has been as it were the *general preparation*. We now come to a more *particular* preparation: and this is fitly ushered in by the Collect, a short prayer which *collects* as it were the needs of the Church, and presents them to God.

293. *I see that the priest reads the Collect with his hands extended. Will you explain the meaning of this act?*

He uses this action in the more solemn prayers, lifting up his hands, like Moses when he prayed against Amalek (*Exod.* xvii. 11). S. Paul alludes to the custom as an adjunct of earnest supplication (1 *Tim.* ii. 8), "that men pray everywhere, *lifting up holy hands*."[1] By this action he spreads as it were the needs of his congregation and of the whole Church before

---

[1] It is not a little singular that the marginal reference is to Malachi i. 11: "And in every place incense shall be offered and a Pure Offering," thus referring this "lifting up holy hands" to the oblation of the Holy Eucharist; and this gathers additional strength when we recall the scope of the Epistle to S. Timothy—an Epistle written *to a bishop* and referring chiefly to questions affecting *the clergy*.

the Lord, as Hezekiah did the letter of Rabshakeh (2 *Kings* xix. 14).

294. *Why is the Epistle read on this side?*

Only because, as a matter of order, the south side is traditionally assigned as the place for reading all Scriptures, except the Gospel, which is read on the north side: the Gospel represents the Christian dispensation, as the Epistle does the Jewish.

295. The changes from south to north, and to the midst of the altar, at the Epistle, Gospel, and Creed, and back again to the Epistle corner for the oblations, are also explained to represent the journeys of our Lord in His Passion from Caiaphas to Pilate, and from Pilate to Herod, and from Herod again to Pilate.

296. *Why does the priest say "Here endeth the Epistle," while he makes no such statement after the Gospel?*

To show that the Jewish dispensation was to cease, while the Gospel is to endure throughout all ages.

297. *The Epistle is sometimes taken from the Old, and sometimes from the New Testament. Can you give me a reason?*

To show that the two Testaments meet in Christ, Who is represented by the Gospel; hence, as Innocent the Third says, the person who reads or sings the Epistle may be said to represent John the Baptist, the forerunner, who closed the line of prophets, and pointed out the

Lamb of God that taketh away the sin of the world. Not unfrequently the Epistle, when taken from the Old Testament, contains the prophecy, the fulfilment of which is recorded by the Gospel, as may be seen in the Holy Week Epistles and Gospels.

298. *The priest says the Creed in the midst of the altar, first extending his hands and saying, " I believe in one God," then joining them again, and saying the rest of the Creed with the server. Will you explain these ceremonies ?*

He goes to the midst of the altar because a more solemn part of the service is now beginning, and because the Creed, as the solemn profession of our faith made in God's presence, is a very direct act of worship to Him. It is begun by the priest and taken up by the people, to show that faith springs from Christ, and through Him is established among the people. Lastly, the priest, having as it were expressed by the spreading out of his hands the solemnity of the action in which he is about to engage, joins them in token of inward recollection, and as a symbol that both priest and people have one common faith.

299. *Why is a reverence made at the words " and was made man," and again at " worshipped and glorified" ?*

In the first place as an acknowledgement of our belief in, and veneration of, our Lord's

Incarnation. To bow the head at this passage is a very ancient custom. The Augustinian Friars first introduced the custom of *kneeling*, which has since become general in the West. In the second case, the reverence expresses our belief in the Divinity of the Holy Ghost. It is probably as old as the Creed itself, the passage being introduced against the heresy of Macedonius, who denied that the Holy Spirit was an object of Divine worship.

300. *The priest now begins the Offertory. What do you understand by the term?*

I understand three things: first, the offerings made by the people, which the server now collects, or receives from some other person, and brings to the priest; secondly, the oblation of the Elements, which now takes place; lastly, the term is used to denote the sentence (more properly called the *Offertory-Antiphon*), which the priest reads after the Creed, while the people are making their offerings.

301. *He reads the sentence still facing the east. Why is this? And please to explain in general why in the greater part of the Celebration he keeps his back to the people?*

I will reply to you in the words of the bishops in their answer to the Puritans in 1661: "The minister's turning to the people is not most convenient throughout the whole ministration. When he speaks to them, as in Lessons, Absolution, and Benedictions, it is convenient that he turn to them; when he speaks for them to God, it is fit that they should all turn another way, as the Ancient Church ever did." This was also the position of the Jewish priest, who ministered "before the Lord" (*Lev.* vi. 7, xxiv. 3) at the altar of incense and at the table of shewbread, i.e. facing the hidden mercy-seat beyond. As to the position being observed in this place, it is sufficient to say that the priest being engaged in an act of ministry before the Lord, although in the presence and on behalf of the people, he only turns from the altar for some weighty cause, and in *direct* addresses to the flock.

302. *Why are the alms, which the priest receives from the server and lays on the altar, almost immediately removed again and placed on the credence?*

The third, fourth, and fifth of the Apostolical Canons forbid that anything be presented upon the altar besides ears of new corn or grapes, and oil for the candlestick, and incense for the time of the holy oblation. And although the alms of the faithful, which are given in lieu of offerings in kind, are fitly offered by the priest, yet it is not expedient that they should remain upon the altar, especially during the oblation and consecration of the Elements.

303. *But are not the "alms" mentioned together with the "oblations" in the prayer for the Church militant?*

Yes: but that does not necessitate their

presence upon the altar at that time. Formerly the bread and wine were offered by the faithful in kind, together with other like offerings, from which indeed the oblations were separated and offered on the altar. The oblations thus included all the offerings, though a part only was offered on the altar. Similarly, the presence of the oblations on the altar serves for the alms, out of which they are wont to be provided.

304. I see that the server in bringing the Elements from the credence, brings wine in his right hand, and water in his left. For what is this water?

To mingle with the wine. This is a most ancient custom, being mentioned by some of the earliest Fathers of the Church, especially by S. Justin Martyr and S. Cyril of Alexandria. Bingham, the ecclesiastical antiquary, by no means a ritualist, testifies to its extreme antiquity.

305. Why is this done?

Partly from a very ancient tradition that the wine was so mingled at the Last Supper, such being the almost universal custom of ancient times: partly from symbolical reasons. Thus it represents the mingled tide of blood and water which flowed from our Saviour's side; and so reminds us (like that) of the two great Sacraments of the Gospel, Baptism and the Eucharist, the latter of which cannot exist without the former. It is likewise symbolical of the Incarnation: the wine as the more precious element representing our Lord's Godhead; the water, as the inferior, His manhood; for which reason and also so as not to impair the nature of the wine, only a few drops of water are added.

306. The priest, before pouring the water into the chalice, blesses it as follows, " By Him mayest thou be blessed, out of whose side there came Blood and Water. In the Name, etc." The bread and wine are not so blessed, because our Lord in appointing them as the essentials of His Sacrifice may be said to have sanctified these elements for their high and holy purpose; while the water (which represents the people), is blessed in order to show the need of the faithful to seek God's sanctifying Spirit in approaching the Eucharist. So to take another symbolism; the wine, as representing the Godhead of Christ, is not blessed, because the Divine Nature stood in no need of sanctification, having been holy from eternity: the water, as representing His manhood, is blessed, to show how He took our fallen nature and sanctified it in the womb of His Mother.

307. *I see that it is said of the element of the Bread that " it shall suffice that it be such as is usual to be eaten, but the best and purest wheat bread that may conveniently be gotten." What is the meaning of this direction?*

The first clause is a *permission* to use unleavened bread, and a declaration of the validity of the Eucharist when so administered; the latter is a cautel or safeguard enjoined from a motive of reverence, as well as to guard against any impurities in the bread, which might endanger the validity of the Sacrament.[1]

308. Anciently *unleavened* bread was invariably used in the West, and was prepared in the form of wafers. This order was continued in the First Prayer Book of Edward VI. In the second, as now, ordinary leavened bread was declared *sufficient*. In the Eastern Church leavened bread is used.[2] The controversy on these respective uses is too intricate to enter into here. It is sufficient to give the *reasons* assigned by either Communion. The Western Church celebrates in unleavened bread (though allowing the *validity* of leavened), because it is believed that our Lord did the same at the Last Supper, when He ate the Passover with His disciples; and because it is fitting that some particular kind of bread should be reserved for so great a Mystery; while the Greek pleads (though by no means clearly) Apostolic tradition; the advantage of showing more distinctly the difference between the Passover and the Eucharist; and the fitness of using the *most perfect kind* of bread (which they assert leavened bread to be) for the Holy Sacrament. As to the *symbolic* use of either, the unleavened bread is held to show the sinlessness of our Lord's human nature, and the purity and spotlessness of the Church, which is His body (see *Heb.* iv. 15; *Eph.* v. 27; i. 22, 23); and so the necessity of each individual Christian to keep himself unspotted from the world, for as S. Paul says, "We being many are one bread, for we are all partakers of that one Bread" (1 *Cor.* x. 17; compare 1 *Cor.* v. 7). On the other hand, the leavened bread,

---

[1] Ordinary baker's bread is often impregnated with foreign substances.

[2] It should be added that the Eastern use of leavened bread differs wholly from ours. In the first place, *leaven* is used, not *yeast*; in the next, the bread is made expressly for the Eucharist in little loaves, an entire one of which is used for every celebration.

like the mixed chalice, is held to represent the two natures of our Lord. That either may lawfully have a symbolic meaning seems clear from the fact that both leavened and unleavened bread was offered with the peace-offering under the Law (*Lev.* vii. 11-13).

309. While then we say with the Council of Florence that "the Body of Christ is truly consecrated in wheaten bread, whether with or without leaven;" and with Theorian, a learned prelate of the Eastern Church, that "if the Divine power transforms the oblations into the Body and Blood of Christ, it is superfluous to dispute whether they were of leavened bread or unleavened bread, of red or of white wine: or to pursue such curious and idle inquiries with respect to these tremendous mysteries;" we would add, with the same Council, that it is more fitting that "every priest should consecrate according to the custom of his Church, be it Eastern or Western;" and that, if leavened bread be used, it is only reverent that it be specially made for the service of the altar, without admixture of foreign matter, and of such consistency as not to crumble, since, as S. Cyril says, "we should most carefully guard lest a crumb fall of that which is more precious than gold or precious stones."[1]

310. *How is the oblation made?*

Custom varies; some priests offering the

---

[1] "Men must not think less to be received in part than in the whole, but in each of them the whole Body of our Saviour Jesu Christ" (*Edward VI's First Prayer Book*). S. Chrysostom, in his letter to Innocent, Bishop of Rome, describing the violence of the soldiers in expelling him from his church, says that they penetrated even where the holy gifts (i.e. the reserved Sacrament) lay; and that the Most Holy Blood of Christ was thrown over the soldiers' coats. In our ordinary use of baker's bread the chancel floor is sometimes strewn with what that "godly bishop" (as the homilies call him) would have called "the most holy flesh of Christ."

elements in either kind separately; others both kinds simultaneously. The same diversity obtained in the mediaeval Church of England; the former usage prevailing in churches which followed the York rite; the latter in those (by far the most numerous), in which the Sarum and Hereford uses were observed. The first is the general usage of the West, the second of the Eastern Church.

311. *Will you explain both these rites?*

In the former case the priest, having received from the server the bread on its dish, takes a sufficient quantity, and putting it on the paten, returns to the midst of the altar, where he elevates it, privately praying the Holy Trinity to accept this oblation at the hands of His unworthy minister; then, having received the wine in like manner, he similarly elevates the chalice, saying privately, "We offer unto Thee, O Lord, the cup of salvation." In the latter case, after having received the elements in both kinds from the server, he places the paten on the top of the chalice, and elevating both together, says the same prayer of oblation, as in the former case over the bread.

312. *What do these rites represent?*

The whole offertory, including both the alms and the oblations, show the duty of honouring God with the first-fruits of our substance (*Prov.* iii. 9), the oblation of the bread and wine being a kind of "meat" (i.e. "food") offering made to God in acknowledgement of our dependence on Him for the fruits of the earth, not less than for the increase of our substance. As a solemn setting apart of the elements to their high and holy end—and so an act having reference to and anticipatory of the consecration—the oblation of the elements refers us to the predetermination of God before all time to work out our salvation by the Incarnation and Death of His Son, "preparing" in His secret council "a Body" as the means of that salvation, when the fullness of time should come. Or as some ritualists have it, as the Consecration shows forth in sacramental verity the sacrifice of the Lord's Death (1 *Cor.* xi. 26), so the anticipatory oblation of the elements shows in symbol the sacrifice of our Lord's life of humiliation, His labours, sorrows, watchings, hunger and the like—which, beginning from the first moment of His conception, had their perfect ending in His last great humiliation even unto the Death of the Cross.[1] The *separate* oblation of the elements here, like their separate consecration hereafter, would signify the parting of our

---

[1] So Goar (in *S. Chrys. Lit. No. 33*) explains the "Great Entrance," which is the corresponding part of the Greek Liturgy. Western ritualists, however, vary the symbolism, saying that our Lord's Advent and Ministry are represented in the *Missa Catechumenorum* ; the former by the Introit, the latter by the Gospel ; and His Passion (as also His Resurrection and Ascension) in the *Missa Fidelium*. According to this view the oblation corresponds to our Lord's delivery by Pilate to be crucified.

Lord's Body and Soul in death, which was the culmination of His life of sacrifice, and so would stand for that whole life now begun to be shown forth: while their being offered *together* here would show the *unity* of the Eucharistic Sacrifice, though offered with two distinct, though not independent, consecrations hereafter.

313. *I see that the priest, after making the oblations, places the chalice on the midst of the altar, and having arranged the paten in front of it, covers the former with a linen veil, and the latter with a corner of the corporal.*[1] *Please to explain these actions.*

He does so primarily to preserve the oblations from dirt, or other danger of irreverence. As a symbolical act, this veiling of the oblations represents either the clothing of the Divinity in substance of our nature at the Incarnation; or, as others take it, our Lord's being clothed in a purple robe and crowned with thorns in the Passion.

314. *Why does the priest return to the epistle corner of the altar, where the server pours a few drops of water over his fingers?*

As a symbol of the purity with which he should approach the Holy Mysteries; for which cause it is customary for him to recite to himself the last six verses of the 26th Psalm

---

[1] The corporal, chalice, paten, etc., are explained in the second section.

during this time; the first word of which in Latin is *Lavabo*, "I will wash," for which reason the ceremony itself came to be known as "the Lavabo." The custom is mentioned by S. Clement, S. Cyril, and other early writers.

315. *What takes place after the Lavabo?*

The priest returns to the middle of the altar, and extending his hands, says: "Let us pray for the whole state of Christ's Church militant here in earth." Then, placing his hands on the altar, he continues the act of oblation down to the words "Thy Divine Majesty"; when he says the rest of the prayer with expanded hands, pausing at the words "sickness or any other adversity," to commemorate privately by name any that need his prayers.

316. *How are we to regard this second oblation?*

It is merely a continuation of the former. The priest having washed his hands, and purified his heart by inward prayer, goes again to the altar, returning as it were with renewed fervour to the act of oblation. In this second act he uses two gestures: first he spreads his hands, and (sometimes) turns towards the people as inviting their co-operation both in the oblation and in the intercessions which accompany it; next he places his hands on the altar to show that it is in dependence on Christ that he ventures to offer the Eucharistic Sacrifice; in the prayer which follows he expands his hands to present, as it were, before heaven the intercessions which he offers.

317. *I think I have seen the priest join his hands after the words " departed in Thy faith and fear." Was this by chance, or had he any reason for doing so ?*

It is an old custom to use this gesture at the private commemoration of the departed, the hands being again expanded when the public recitation of the prayer is resumed.

The English Liturgy, like the Roman, the Ambrosian, and the Ethiopic, has *two* commemorations of the departed, one before, the other after the consecration. The first answers to the Commemoration of departed Saints; the second to the "Memento" or prayer for the dead in general. Various reasons are assigned by Western ritualists for the placing of the Commemoration of the living *before* and that of the departed *after* the Consecration, which thus, like Aaron of old, stands between the living and the dead, bringing to each the blessings needful to their respective conditions. It may be observed, too, that the two commemorations of the dead, together with that of the living, include the whole Church of Christ, both that portion of it "militant here in earth" and that which rests "from its labours," whether in the courts of heaven—the Church Triumphant—or in the intermediate state—the living, the saints, the dead in general. On the second Commemoration of the Departed, see further paragraph 385 below.

318. *Whom should the priest remember at the pause after these words ?*

He should at least call to mind the Saint, if any, whom the Church that day commemorates, and the Saint in whose honour the particular church is dedicated; with others whom his devotion may suggest, as the patron of the diocese, and the like. The Eastern liturgies first make mention of "the Fathers, Patriarchs, Prophets, Apostles, Preachers, Evangelists, Martyrs, Confessors, Virgins, and every just spirit made perfect;" and then go on to mention specially by name "the Mother of God and ever Virgin Mary; the holy prophet John, the forerunner and Baptist," the Saint of the day, "and all Thy Saints." The Roman order agrees with this in mentioning the Blessed Virgin first, and concluding with "All Saints," but commemorates with these the twelve Apostles, and twelve principal Martyrs of the early Church.

319. Formerly the names of those to be prayed for in the Liturgy were written on tablets, or parchments, which, from being folded twice, were called the *diptychs*: and in these the same threefold division was observed. The first column contained the name of the Patriarch, Archbishop, and Bishop, of the reigning Emperor, and of the benefactors of the Church; the second a list of the Saints specially honoured there; the third the names of those who had fallen asleep in Christ.

320. *Why does the priest mention the names of those for whom he wishes to pray in secret rather than aloud?*

It is a very old custom for the priest to say certain prayers in the Liturgy in that way, especially the Commemorations; perhaps to stir himself up to greater recollection, or because these prayers were of a more private nature, and so it was not necessary for the people to follow them, but rather to be occupied with their own private devotions. Sometimes he prays aloud, in imitation of our Lord, Who spake aloud the seven words from the Cross; at others, like Hannah, he "speaks in" his "heart, only" his "lips move, but" his "voice is not heard" (1 *Sam.* i. 13). This, while it gives the people an opportunity of offering the Sacrifice for their own intentions,[1] or to exercise themselves in private prayer, is not without symbolical teaching; both as representing the two kinds of prayer, vocal and mental, in which Christians are wont to engage, and as showing that here upon earth we see the mysteries of God "through a glass darkly," believing with an entire faith, but only partially comprehending.

321. *Why does the priest turn toward the people when he says the Exhortation, "Ye that do truly"?*

He now breaks off the Sacrifice, as it were, to prepare the communicants. Hence he turns to those whom he is addressing.

322. *Why is he directed to address "them that come to receive the Holy Communion"?*

Because the acts that follow are intended to prepare the communicants, and therefore do

---

[1] Intentions are the particular objects which we wish to gain (whether for ourselves or others) by any act of devotion. Thus the Lord's Prayer is said by the people at a Baptism to obtain the grace of perseverance for the newly-baptized infant.

not refer to those who are present only to worship.

323. *Perhaps this is the reason for a custom which I have noticed in some churches, for the communicants alone to say the Confession which follows. Am I right in this supposition?*

Perfectly so. The Exhortation shows that the Confession and Absolution refer chiefly, at all events, to "those that are minded to receive." I may remark, however, that the rubric orders the Confession to be made "by one of the ministers" (i.e. the server at Low Celebration), "in the name of the communicants, evidently intending him to recite it *alone*. There is, however, no objection to the communicants (or indeed the whole congregation) joining him in this act.

324. This rubric is an incidental proof of the Church's desire to retain pre-Reformation usages when they are such as not, in her judgement, to involve erroneous teaching. For by the use of the word "minister" here, she implies that the custom of having a lay server in the numerous cases in which there was only one priest, was to be retained; while in the employment of the general phrase "one of the ministers," she points to the full or solemn celebration with deacon and subdeacon (who were technically called the *ministri* [1])—the solemnizing "these high and holy mysteries with all the suffrages and due order appointed for the same," as Edward VI's First Book worded it. So also the direction to the minister to say it [alone] "in the

---

[1] A term which included, however, the taper-bearers, thurifer, and acolyte.

name of " the communicants, was quite in accordance with the idea that the server, or the ministers and choir, represented and acted for the people.[1]

325. *I should like you to explain one or two things in connection with the Absolution. And first, is it (as the name would seem to imply) a loosing from sin?*

It is no doubt designed as a *ritual* cleansing of those who are to feast upon the Sacrifice; and if joined with true sorrow, does convey or rather seal pardon for those lesser faults of human frailty which destroy not, though they impair, the grace of God in the soul. When united with a firm sorrow and desire for amendment, it bears the same relation to sacramental absolution as spiritual does to actual Communion.[2] It would seem to be called "the Absolution" in a more general sense, rather than in the strict sense in which theologians use the word, when it is employed to represent

---

[1] It is not meant that the Church contemplates a *dumb* attendance at the Holy Eucharist on the part of the people —the "parson and clerk" theory of Divine worship—but that they represent in their ministerial *acts* the people's participation in offering the sacrifice with and at the hands of the priest. At the same time I am not sorry for the opportunity of hinting to those whom it may concern that *noisy* responses are specially out of place in a Low Celebration, the leading idea of which is *stillness*, and reverent quiet, just as that of a High or Choral Celebration is a jubilant rejoicing before the Lord; though even then the music should be of a softer and more subdued character than that employed for the Psalter.

[2] Spiritual Communion is described and explained in paragraph 380.

a sacramental act composed of several distinct parts—all of which, except a form of words, invoking God's pardon and forgiveness, are here wanting.

326. Yet the priest would seem to use it "as one having authority." He extends his hand towards the people, as in blessing, and makes the sign of the Cross over them.

The prayer called the Absolution is undoubtedly a solemn benediction at the hand of God's minister, and as such should be reverently and thankfully received; and to those who feel themselves in dispositions of grace, it is a *seal* and *earnest* of the pardon they have already obtained; and a means of deepening and quickening their sorrow for past sin. Indeed, an Absolution, in the *liturgical* sense of the word, differs but little from a benediction except in the kind of blessings it invokes. Its exact quasi-sacramental value cannot be very rigidly defined.

327. Formerly the Confession and the first part of the Absolution were interchanged between priest and people, the priest adding the last clause. The same was done at Prime and Compline. In the same way at Matins the first lesson of each nocturn was preceded by an "Absolution," as every lesson was by a benediction. Of these one only (that for the third nocturn on Sundays and festivals, and for the ferial nocturn on Tuesdays and Saturdays), contained any allusion to the remission of sins: "From the chain of our sins may the almighty and merciful Lord absolve us." The other two are merely benedictions with a slight

I

penitential aspect: "Hear our prayers and *pity* us;" "God of His merciful kindness *help* us." The form at Prime and Compline, and in the Mass, was that now used in the Communion Service, omitting the clause: "Our heavenly Father . . . and true faith turn to Him," and ending at "everlasting life."

328. *How does the priest resume the Sacrifice?*

He turns to the altar and says the Preface, or introduction to the Canon, i.e. the Consecration. But as a preparation for this more solemn part of the Liturgy he first says, elevating his hands: "Lift up your hearts;" the people replying: "We lift them up unto the Lord." Then joining his hands in meek acknowledgement of the Divine mercies, he says: "Let us give thanks unto our Lord God;" to which the people answer "It is meet and right so to do."

329. *Explain these sentences?*

In the first the priest invites us to withdraw our attention wholly from the things of earth, that we may join with angels and archangels in offering the Divine Oblation. The people in their reply assert their readiness to do so. He next bids us begin our offering with the giving of thanks, which we acknowledge to be meet and right. In the Preface, the priest as it were catches up and amplifies this our acknowledgement, declaring it "very meet, right, and our bounden duty," "at all times and in all places" to "give thanks" to God.

330. *What are the "Proper" Prefaces?*

They are clauses in which we specially commemorate, at certain seasons, particular mercies, for which it is fitting to give thanks at that time

331. *What are these seasons?*

The octaves of Christmas, Easter, Ascension, and Whitsun Days, and the feast of the Holy Trinity. The service for the Coronation of the Sovereign has also a Proper Preface.

332. *Why are the words "Holy Father" omitted on Trinity Sunday?*

Because the Preface is then addressed specially to God as the One in Three, not as at other times to the Father alone.

333. *What is the* Sanctus?

It is a very ancient hymn of the Church taken from Isaiah vi. 3. The threefold repetition of the epithet "Holy" (which occurs also *Rev.* iv. 8) has ever been regarded as an acknowledgement of the doctrine of the Holy Trinity. It occurs also in the *Te Deum*. It is called the *Sanctus* from the first word in the Latin: sometimes the *Ter Sanctus*, or *thrice holy*, from the threefold repetition of the word. The Greeks also call it the *Epinikion*, or "triumphal hymn."

334. *Why do the people join in at the* Sanctus?

In imitation of the heavenly host, of whom we

read that "one cried unto another, and said: Holy, holy, holy."

335. This part of the service is of extreme antiquity, and occurs in every Liturgy extant. The Preface and *Sanctus* are mentioned by Tertullian (*de Orat.*), S. Cyprian (*de Orat. Dom.*), S. Cyril of Jerusalem (*Catech. Myst.* 5), the Apostolical Constitutions (l. v. c. 16), S. Chrysostom, the Sacramentaries of Gelasius and S. Gregory, etc.

336. *Why is a bell rung at the* Sanctus *?*

To stir up the people to join in this triumphal hymn with especial devotion, and also to give notice that the Canon or more solemn part of the service is about to commence.[1]

337. *I notice that the priest at the beginning of the Preface disjoins his hands; and at the* Sanctus *joins them before his breast. What is the meaning of these gestures?*

They represent the varied dispositions with which he says the Preface. The disjoined hands signify that at all times and in all places it is meet and right to praise God; the priest's hands are joined before the breast because he unites himself in the *Sanctus* with the heavenly host,

---

[1] The bell rung is sometimes a small handbell rung by the server, at other times the sacristan rings one of the church bells—generally one hung over the chancel for this purpose, and hence called the *Sanctus-bell*, *Sancte-bell*, or *Service-bell*. The latter bell was generally rung at the parochial Mass to enable such of the parishioners as were prevented from attending the service to join in it in spirit. Sanctus-bell cotes remain in many of our churches, and the bell itself in some, as Long Compton, Warwickshire, and Claydon, Suffolk.

and with the people; at the same time he bows as with them, in adoration of the Divine Majesty. The words "Blessed is He that cometh in the Name of the Lord. Hosanna in the highest," which are sometimes added to the *Sanctus* are a restoration of a clause which forms part of the hymn in nearly every ancient Liturgy, Eastern or Western, and which was retained in our English "Mass" of 1549.

338. Do not these minute acts tend to disturb the priest? An attention to such trifles must, I imagine, be very distracting; they seem to me to be too insignificant to demand his care.

In the service of God nothing can be trivial or insignificant, or beneath the notice of those who are appointed to conduct it. You will find that the most spiritual among the holy men of old whom the Church commemorates were remarkable for the care which they exercised over the minutest details of Divine worship. As for their tending to disturb the priest, they have a precisely opposite effect. They help him to realize the acts in which he is engaged. Besides which, as long as we are in the flesh we must worship with the body, as well as with the spirit and understanding; and as *some* posture must be employed, it is more seemly to follow a fixed tradition than to act haphazard. Lastly, by prescribing gestures, the Church helps to preserve true doctrine and the idea of worship in both priest and people.

339. Whence it was that Bucer, who wished to protestantize the English Church, and to remove every mark of her inherent Catholicity from her Prayer Book, objected to the retention of the "gestures"—*nunquam satis execrandae Missae gestus*, as he styles them.

340. *What is the prayer which the priest says kneeling at the midst of the altar?*

It is a humble acknowledgement of his own unworthiness to execute the ministry which he is about to perform, and of that of the communicants to join with him in the Sacrifice by feasting on the Sacred Victim Who is now about to be offered. Whence it is called the "Prayer of Humble Access" or the "Prayer of Address," as the Coronation Service has it.

341. *Why are the communicants alone mentioned here?*

Because in the primitive ages all the faithful, i.e. all baptized Christians not under discipline, were in the habit of communicating with the priest; a godly discipline, which the Church wishes it were possible to be now observed.

342. *Does the Church, then, contemplate the presence of none but those who are going to communicate?*

I have already shown you that this is not the case by the direction to the priest to address certain exhortations specially to those of the congregation "who are minded to receive the Holy Communion." The Church does not contemplate the departure of any of her baptized children, till the priest "lets them depart" with the final benediction.

343. Bucer, whose opposition to the Sacrifice is mentioned above, yet did not venture to deny that the Eucharist was the appointed and especial way of keeping holy Sunday and the festivals of the Church. He even wished to make it *compulsory* on all persons to communicate at these times, as the Church was wont to *require* all to "hear Mass." But he happily failed to carry his point. People were still left at liberty to "receive" or to "be present," as they judged it better to their soul's health.

344. *Why is the Prayer of Consecration called the "Canon"?*

From a Greek word signifying "the rule," because it embodies the unchanging form to be used everywhere in offering the Eucharistic Sacrifice: and which was not left to the discretion of the bishop or priest, as much of the other parts of the service was in early times.

345. *Why is the priest to say it "standing before the" altar?*

Because this is the position of a sacrificing priest (*Rev.* v. 6; *Heb.* x. 11). See also paragraph 301.

346. *Why is the altar here and elsewhere called the Lord's Table?*

Because from it the Sacred Mysteries are dispensed. The Jewish altar was so called (*Mal.* i. 7), and the altars at which heathen sacrifices were offered were similarly called "tables" (1 *Cor.* x. 21).

347. The Christian altar is also our *table of Showbread* (*Exod.* xxv. 23, 30; *Heb.* ix. 2). Bishop Andrewes says: "The Holy Eucharist being considered as a sacrifice, it is fitly called an altar, which again is fitly called a table, the Eucharist being considered as a sacrament." This twofold character of the Christian altar accounts for its being made of *wood* or *stone* indifferently. In the Eastern Church the altar is called the "Holy Table," or "Lord's Table." In Edward VI's First Prayer Book it was styled "God's Board." In the Coronation Service both terms, "Altar" and "Lord's Table," are employed.

348. *Of what does the Canon consist?*

Of the Commemoration of the Passion, the Invocation, and the Consecration Proper.

349. *What is the Commemoration of the Passion?*

The first part of the Canon, down to the words "until His coming again."

350. *What is the Invocation?*

The part of the Canon beginning: "Hear us, O merciful Father," down to "may be partakers of His most blessed Body and Blood."

351. *What is the Consecration Prayer?*

The words, "This is My Body"—"This is My Blood," are the words by which the Consecration is effected; but the last part of the Canon, beginning at "Who in the same night," is called the Consecration.

352. *Why does the priest uncover the oblations at the end of the Invocation?*

To prepare them for the Consecration which follows. As a symbolical act, this unveiling represents the stripping off of our Lord's garments at the crucifixion.

353. *Does the priest do anything else in preparation for the Consecration?*

Yes, he first separates his hands, and then gently rubs the thumb and forefinger of each within the corporal. He does so to free them from any grain of dust or other substance that may have adhered to them since the lavabo, and also in token of reverence due to the Sacred Mysteries he is about to celebrate.

354. *Will you explain the other actions connected with the Canon?*

He begins it with his hands expanded, in token of supplication, and with eyes lifted up to the Father in heaven, before whom he is offering the Holy Oblation; at the Invocation he spreads the palms of his hands over the oblations, as it were calling down upon them the Divine benediction; for which reason he makes the sign of the Cross over each element as he mentions it by name; in the other actions he imitates, as near as may be, our Lord's own gestures, taking the paten into his hands when he says, " He took "; breaking the bread when he says, " He brake it." He lays his hands on either element as he pronounces the words of consecration, in imitation of the Jewish priests, who were wont to lay their hands on the head of the victim.

355. *Does he use any other gestures in the Canon?*

Yes; he bows down over the altar at the words, "Who in the same night"; at the words "When He had given thanks" he makes the sign of the Cross over the paten with his right hand; and directly he has pronounced the words of consecration, "This is My Body," he genuflects; he elevates the larger wafer or bread at the words "Do this in remembrance of Me." Similarly, at the consecration of the chalice, he makes the sign of the Cross at the words "When He had given thanks"; immediately after the words "This is My Blood," he genuflects; then, rising, he elevates the chalice, as he finishes the consecration prayer.

356. *Why does he bow down over the altar?*

To show the recollection and fervour with which he should engage in the solemn act of consecration.

357. *Why does he make the sign of the Cross over the paten at the words "when He had given thanks"?*

To imitate more closely the action of our Lord, Who, before He "brake" the bread, "blessed" it (*S. Matt.* xxvi. 26).

In the old English Liturgies, and in the First Prayer Book of Edward VI, the words ran " when He had *blessed* and given thanks He brake it "; and there was no direction to the priest to break the Bread at that time. The word " blessed " was omitted in 1552 —why it does not appear—and the direction as to fraction inserted at the last revision of the Prayer Book in 1662.

358. *Why does he genuflect after each consecration ?*

In lowliest worship of our Lord, now present under the forms of bread and wine.

359. *Ought we, then, to worship Christ in the Sacrament ?*

Yes; as God He is to be worshipped, whereever and under whatever conditions He vouchsafes to manifest Himself. " We adore and worship Christ in the Eucharist," says Bishop Ridley, who died for the reformed faith; "we behold with the eyes of faith Him present after grace, and spiritually set on the table; and we worship Him that sitteth above, and is worshipped of angels." So also Bishop Forbes: "Christ in the Eucharist is to be adored with Divine worship, inasmuch as His living and glorified Body is present therein." And again, the devout Bishop Jeremy Taylor: "Place thyself upon thy knees in the devoutest and humblest position of worshippers, and think it not much in the lowest manner to worship the King of men and angels, the Lord of heaven and earth, the great lover of souls, and the

Saviour of the body; Him whom all the angels of God worship. . . . For if Christ be not there after a peculiar manner, whose body do we receive? But if He be present not in mystery only, but in blessing also, why do we not worship? But all the Christians always did so from time immemorial."

360. *Does not the Twenty-eighth Article say that the Sacrament of the Lord's Supper is not to be worshipped? And the declaration at the end of the Communion Service, that no adoration is intended, or ought to be done to the Sacramental Bread and Wine, or to any corporal presence of Christ's natural Flesh and Blood? How do these statements accord with what you have said above?*

The Twenty-eighth Article says that our Lord ordained the Sacrament not for the purpose of being worshipped, but of being received. It condemns those who professed great reverence for the Blessed Sacrament by constantly being present for purposes of *worship*, whether at the celebration of the Eucharist, and especially when it was *lifted up* for the worship of the faithful; or in presence of it when *received*; or when it was *carried* to the sick or in processions: and yet neglected *the very end and aim* of its institution, its frequent reception by all the faithful. S. Chrysostom had done the same 1,100 years before. The "Declaration" denies that adoration is due to the Sacramental Bread and Wine, which are but the *veils* which shroud our Lord, and as such are no more to be worshipped than were His *clothes* when He was upon earth; or to any *corporal* presence of Christ's *natural* Flesh and Blood; for His presence is not after a corporal or natural manner, but after the manner of a Sacrament.[1]

361. *What do you mean by "after the manner of a Sacrament"?*

I mean a supernatural and mysterious manner which it is impossible for us to understand while we see through a glass darkly. Just as our Lord's Body after His resurrection passed, contrary to the nature of His natural Body, through closed doors, so that same Body, seated on the Father's right hand in heaven, is yet present on our altars, not *corporally* or by way of location, as moving from one place to another, but by extension. We cannot understand how His Godhead remained in heaven, and yet took flesh in Mary's womb; neither can we understand how His whole Nature, Manhood, and Godhead, is now in heaven, and yet is truly present on our altars.

---

[1] A truth which the Catechism of the Council of Trent affirms with equal clearness: "The Body of Christ cannot be rendered present by change of place, as it would then cease to be in heaven; for whatever is moved, must of necessity cease to occupy the place from which it is moved." Part ii, ch. iv, q. 39. And again at greater length Quest. 42: "The Body of our Lord present in the Eucharist not as in a place," or by way of *location*.

362. *But why does the priest worship after each consecration?*

I might answer you in the words of Bishop Poynet, that "the Flesh of Christ is to be adored, although a creature, by reason of the Divinity to which it is united." The Blood of Christ, although a creature, is worthy of adoration. But, in truth, these cannot be separated from His Divinity. Wheresoever the Flesh of Christ is, there is He Himself, *whole and entire*, His Body, His Blood, His Soul and Godhead; and as such He is worshipped, whether under the form of Bread or of Wine. But the twofold adoration has also a *theological* meaning. The separate consecration of each element represents the separation of our Lord's Soul and Body on the Cross, which was the consummation of His Sacrifice. By the twofold consecration the priest shows forth this crowning act of sacrifice by way of memorial before God; by his twofold adoration he expresses the truth that "Christ being dead, dieth no more"; that the sacrifice on Calvary was His one oblation of Himself with "shedding of blood," of which the Eucharist is the true, but unbloody, memorial.

363. *But does not this justify communion in One kind?*

It shows that such a communion is a real and efficacious participation of Christ, and so justifies it in *extreme* cases. Thus the early Church was wont to communicate infants in the species of wine alone, the sweet taste of which induced them to swallow it readily; while she sent the Communion in the form of bread alone to the confessors in prison at the times of persecution, when a priest could not be had to consecrate for them in the prison. But it is very far from justifying it as a *general* use, in the face of the institution of our Saviour, as interpreted by the universal custom of the Church (except in the extreme cases I have mentioned), and of the doctrine of the best divines even of the Roman Church, that either species in the Blessed Sacrament has its own special grace.[1]

364. The Act passed at Westminster, in December, 1547, for the receiving of the Blessed Sacrament "in both kyndes," and the subsequent proclamation attached to the "Order of Communion," recognize possible occasions of Communion under one kind, enacting "that the most blessed Sacrament of the Body and Blood of our Saviour Christ should from henceforth be commonly delivered and ministered unto all persons within our realm of England and Ireland, and other our dominions, under both kinds, that is to say, of bread and wine (*except necessity otherwise require*)."

365. *Why does he elevate the Blessed Sacrament after either Consecration?*

For two reasons: first, as presenting the Sacrifice to the Father under the separate forms which represent His Soul and Body parted in death; and as showing the Lord's death before

---
[1] See authorities quoted in Dr. Pusey's *Letter to the Bishop of London*, pp. 162, 163. Third Edition. 1851.

the people by this act; and again, as exhibiting to them Christ really though invisibly present to receive their homage. In this the priest imitates S. John the Baptist, who was not content with worshipping his Lord, but pointed Him out to the people, saying "Behold the Lamb of God."

366. Whence the rite was called the "Elevation," or *lifting up*, viewed under the first aspect; the "Ostension," or *showing*, viewed under the second. Both are met with in the ancient liturgies of the East. Thus the Liturgy of S. James mentions in its very form of Consecration the elevation as done to God, and asserts that our Lord used this gesture at the first Eucharist: "Taking bread in His holy, spotless, blameless, and immortal hands, looking up to heaven, *and showing it to Thee, His God and Father*, giving thanks, hallowing, breaking it, He gave it to His disciples," etc. So in the Liturgy of S. Chrysostom, the priest, "elevating the holy Bread, says, Holy things for holy persons," and soon after the deacon takes the chalice reverently, and advances to the door (of the screen), and "elevating the holy Chalice, *shows it to the people*."

367. In the "Order of Communion," 1548, the elevation was forbidden at a *second* Consecration of the Chalice. The First Prayer Book of Edward VI, issued the next year, went further, directing the *main* Consecration to be effected "without any elevation, or showing the Sacrament to the people." Both these orders were apparently directed against the theories of Transubstantiation and the *local* presence of Christ —and so against the *ostension* to the people, not the *elevation* to God. The prohibition was removed in the Second Prayer Book two years and a half later, and has not been since revived. Bishop Wren, among others, was wont to use this symbolical action.

368. Liturgical writers see also in the elevation a ritual representation of the lifting up of our Lord on the Cross, and apply to the attractive grace which flows alike from the Passion and from the Eucharist, which is its memorial, that saying of our Saviour's: "I, if *I be lifted up*, will draw all men unto Me."

369. *Why does the bell ring again at the elevation?*

To inform the people who might not hear the words or see the actions of the celebrant that the Consecration has taken place, and to stir them up to worship Christ with the priest in His Sacramental Presence.

370. The bell used is generally that employed at the *Sanctus*, whence it used also to be known as the *sacring-bell* (sacring being the old English word for consecration). When, however, a bell suspended over the chancel was used for the former, the large bell of the church was generally rung at the Consecration to mark the dignity of that crowning act of the Service.

371. *Why does the priest pray in silence after the Consecration?*

To prepare himself for the reception of the Blessed Sacrament. He continues standing, because his communion is an essential part of the Sacrifice. Mystically these "silent prayers" represent the stillness of the tomb in which our Lord lay after His crucifixion. They also show the reverence due to the Mystical Presence on the altar. "The Lord is in His holy temple: let all the earth *keep silence* before Him."

372. Is there not a custom of making a second fraction of the Bread after the Consecration?

Yes; the priest divides the Host, from which he broke a small particle before Consecration, into two portions; he drops the small particle into the chalice. Traces of the fraction before Consecration are found in several Missals, for instance, a Reims Missal of 1572 contains the rubric, *While saying* He brake, *he breaks the host slightly;* but the breaking after Consecration has been from time immemorial, and still is, the important symbolical fraction in all Liturgies. [B.]

373. The "fraction" occurs in every liturgy, but the number of parts varies. The Liturgy of S. James directs a division of the Host into *two*; that of S. Chrysostom into *four*; the old English liturgies, like that of the West in general, into *three*. The threefold division is held to symbolize the three divisions of the Church at the time of our Lord's Resurrection — the Court of heaven, the spirits in prison to whom our Lord preached (1 S. *Pet.* iii. 19) in Hades, and the faithful on earth. The placing of the portion in the chalice is explained as symbolical of our Lord's descent into hell, and also that the Church militant is as it were plunged into the chalice, that is, made to partake of our Lord's sufferings. Or, as some explain it better, the separate consecration of our Lord's Body and Soul in the act of death, this commixture is emblematical of their *reunion* at the Resurrection.

374. Why does the priest again genuflect before communicating himself?

As an acknowledgement of his own unworthiness. He communicates standing, as I have said, because his communion is an essential part of the Sacrifice (*Lev.* vi. 26), and *standing* the sacrificial position.

375. *I notice that in communicating the people the priest begins at the Epistle side; and that, if the server communicates, he administers to him first of all. Why is this?*

The people are communicated from *left* to *right*, possibly,[1] to show the progress in holiness which these mysteries should produce: "They will go from strength to strength" (*Ps.* lxxxiv. 7), as David says in a Psalm which spiritual writers has always applied to the Blessed Sacrament. The server is communicated first, because he represents the choir at a Low Celebration; and those in choir, first the clergy and then the lay members, were wont to receive first; afterwards those in the body of the church, first the clergy, and then the laity in order. He also represents the sacred ministers (i.e. the deacon and subdeacon), who, as actually engaged in the Sacrifice, communicated immediately after the priest.

376. Anciently the people were communicated in the body of the church, first the men, who sat on the south, or *Epistle* side; afterwards the women, on the north, or *Gospel* side.

377. The order as to precedency in communicating

---

[1] That is, left to right of the priest as he faces the people in the act of distribution.

the people is of great antiquity, and was probably observed from the first. The communion of the clergy according to their rank is referred to in the 18th Canon of the Council of Nice. In the Eastern Liturgies the priest communicates the deacon (without whom no Celebration takes place) in the Bread immediately after his own reception in that kind; and similarly in the Chalice; afterwards the people in order, the men first, then the women.

378. *Are there any other ceremonies connected with the Communion of the people ?*

Yes; and first, the gestures of the communicants at the moment of reception. These I will describe in the words of S. Cyril, who wrote in the fourth century: " Approaching therefore, come not with thy wrists extended, or thy fingers open; but make thy left hand as it were a throne for thy right, which is on the eve of receiving the King; and having hollowed thy palm receive the Body of Christ, saying after It 'Amen.' Give heed lest thou lose any of It, for what thou losest is a loss to thee as from thine own members. . . . Then approach to the Cup of His Blood, not stretching forth thy hands, but bending, and saying in the way of worship and reverence, 'Amen,' be thou hallowed by partaking also of the Blood of Christ." S. John Damascene alludes to the same custom, but sees in the crossed palms a symbol of our Lord's Passion. " Placing our palms in the form of a cross, let us receive the Body of the Crucified." The other custom is to spread a towel or linen cloth over the rails at the Communion of the people. This is done to guard the more effectually against the falling of any portion of the Blessed Sacrament to the ground. Sometimes the server and some other official of the church hold this towel before the communicants. (See par. 53.)

379. In the First Liturgy of Edward VI the modern Roman custom of communicating the people *in their mouths* was continued, though the antiquity of the present form was recognized. In the second Liturgy the priest was directed to deliver the Communion to the people "in their hands." The communion-cloth is still a part of the statutable furniture of chancels, and was ordered to be used at the Coronation of George IV.

380. *Do not those who are not going to communicate sometimes make an act of Spiritual Communion during the administration of the Sacrament?*

Yes; in token of their desire to communicate; and in imitation of the woman who touched the hem of our Lord's garment (*S. Matt.* ix. 20, xiv. 36). It is done by making *acts* (or short exercises) of faith, hope, and charity, and of ardent desire to receive our Lord, followed by a short invitation to Him to come at least and visit us spiritually, since we cannot now (either through our unworthiness, or from any other cause—as having already communicated at an earlier celebration) receive Him sacramentally. Its introduction here is a sign that we are one body with those of our brethren who are privileged to approach the altar; and serves to remind us that it is only the sins and imperfections of our own hearts which hinder us from a more frequent, or even a *daily* participation in those heavenly mysteries.

381. *When all have communicated, the priest covers the chalice and paten with a fair linen cloth. Will you explain this act?*

It is in principle the same as the corresponding veiling of the oblations at the Offertory (see par. 313); only it is done with greater solemnity, as being performed to God incarnate under the sacramental veils. Symbolically, it represents the veiling or hiding of our Lord's Divinity when He stooped to taste death: or His being wrapped in a linen cloth at His burial.

382. *What is the Post-Communion Prayer?*

It is a collect said by the priest after the Communion, begging God to accept our Sacrifice. Such a petition occurs in every Liturgy, sometimes before, sometimes immediately after the Consecration; or as here after the Communion of the people.[1] The Communion of priest and people having *completed* the Sacrifice,

---

[1] The *second* prayer should never be said, unless the priest has said the *first* in his "private prayers" after Consecration, the place it occupied in Edward VI's First Liturgy, and where Bishop Overall was accustomed to say it; or (which seems allowable) says *both* prayers here. Otherwise the Canon is not complete.

the Church again offers it to the Father for "all the whole Church."

383. *Will you explain the phrase* "all *the* whole *Church"? It appears to be a needless repetition, since the* "*whole*" *must include* "*all.*"

It is an instance of the figure of speech called "Pleonasm," which employs words in themselves superfluous for the sake of greater emphasis. A similar figure is employed by the Church in the Psalter, in which, on account of His supernal exaltation far above every creature, God is called "the *Most* High*est.*" It is here used to show the *universal* application of the Sacrifice, the benefits of which permeate as it were through *the entire* mystical body of Christ. As Bishop Andrewes says, it "is available for present, absent, living, dead; yea, even for them that are yet unborn." In other words, by this phrase the Sacrifice is pleaded for the threefold divisions of the Church—militant, expectant, and triumphant —the faithful on earth, the saints departed, and the dead in general.

384. *Please to explain two things. First, why should we pray for the Saints, who await with certainty the fruition of glory? And if it be lawful to pray for them, how can we ask for them* "*remission of all their sins*"?

The most ancient Liturgies offer the Sacrifice on behalf of the Saints, even of the Blessed

Virgin—not to obtain for them remission of sins, but increase of glory; and above all, that final consummation of glory, when their souls shall be reunited to the risen and glorified body. The prayer asks for each division of the Church the benefits suited to its condition: for *us* "remission of all our sins," and whatever else we stand in need of; for *them* the "benefits of Christ's Passion," in so far as it can affect them now, which is by increasing their happiness, and augmenting their joy, and by hastening the accomplishment of the number of God's elect.

385. *Whom should the priest mention at the pause here?*

Those whom he wishes to commemorate of the faithful dead; since he has already made mention of the two other classes at the Oblation. (See par. 318.)

386. *What is the meaning of the phrase " Sacrifice of praise and thanksgiving" in this prayer?*

It is a translation of the term, *Sacrificium laudis*, which occurs in the Roman and old English Mass, and was applied also to the Jewish Sacrifices (*Amos* iv. 5; *Jer*. xxxiii. 11), not as being a Sacrifice of our praise and thanksgiving merely, but a Sacrifice "*offered for a thanksgiving*" (*Lev*. vii. 12). "It is a Sacrifice of praise and thanksgiving," says

Thorndike, "because it is contained in those kinds" (or elements) "of Bread and Wine, which served for meat and drink offerings in the law of Moses."

387. *Is there any other phrase in this prayer that demands explanation?*

Yes; the priest styles the ministry in which he has been engaged "this our bounden duty and service"—*obsequium servitutis meæ*, as a somewhat similar prayer in the Roman Mass words it—a phrase which, like the word MASS (see par. 285), expresses the truth that the Eucharistic Sacrifice is the great act of homage due from man to his Creator; not left to his choice or caprice, but his *bounden duty*.

388. *This I suppose is the reason that the congregation, in churches where ritual has been restored, remain to the end of the Communion service?*

Yes; the Church has ever required the presence of her children at these Mysteries on each Lord's Day; to which were afterwards added sundry other feasts, thence called *feasts of obligation*.

389. The *Days of Obligation* in the present Continental Church vary in different countries, they generally include, in addition to all Sundays in the year, the feasts of Christmas, Circumcision, Epiphany, and Ascension, Corpus Christi, SS. Peter and Paul, the Assumption, and All Saints' Day, with an obligation to *communicate* "at Easter," which Canonists explain

to apply to any time between Palm Sunday (or even the beginning of Lent), and the Octave of Easter. In the English Church the *obligation of communicating* is extended to "*three times* in the year, of which Easter is to be one" (the other two, according to old custom, being Christmas and Whitsuntide). Various local synods from time to time increased the feasts of obligation within their own bounds. It is doubtful whether the Church of England intended her children to regard as "days of obligation" *all* the feasts mentioned as "to be observed" in the Table of Feasts appended to the Calendar. But it is of course a pious custom to assist at the Holy Eucharist, with or without communicating, on these days.

390. *Why is the hymn "Glory be to God on high" said after the Post-Communion?*

Probably in imitation of our Lord and His Apostles, who after the first Eucharist "sang an hymn."[1] In the Eastern Church this hymn is sung at Matins; in the West, at an earlier stage of the Mass, before the Collect, Epistle, and Gospel for the day. It continued to hold this position in the first Liturgy of Edward VI. In its original position ritualists saw in it a representation of the birth of Christ, as in the Introit of His Advent. In its present place it may show forth our joy at the Resurrection, which is represented by this part of the Service.

---

[1] S. Matt. xxvi. 30; S. Mark xiv. 26. The marginal reading is "psalm," and it ought to be added that there is a tradition (endorsed by Bishop Jer. Taylor, *Life of Christ*, p. iii, sec. 15), that our Lord and His Apostles sang the "greater Hallel," consisting of Psalms cxiii to cxviii. These six Psalms are still sung by the Jews at their annual festivals, and especially after the Passover and at the Feast of Tabernacles.

391. It was formerly omitted on those penitential seasons when the *Te Deum* was not said (see par. 230), on account of its joyful character; whence a custom obtains in some churches of *saying* it plain at those times (i.e. without music), even in Choral Celebrations.

392. *Why is the priest directed to* "let *the people* depart" *with the final blessing?*

Formerly in this place the deacon, turning towards the people, chanted aloud "Ite, Missa est," "Go, the liturgy is over;" the people, however, remaining for the priest's benediction, which followed soon after; and, if possible, not departing till the priest had returned into the vestry. The benediction consists of two parts— "The Peace of God" and the Benediction proper.

393. *What do these represent?*

They serve to remind us of the apparitions of our Lord after His Resurrection, when He said to His disciples "Peace be unto you"; and His "lifting up His hands, and blessing them," as He was taken up from them into heaven. Thus pious writers have seen in the Eucharistic celebration a mystical representation of our Lord's life and Sacrifice,[1] from the first moment of His Conception until His Ascension into heaven and His session at the right hand of God, where He offers, by way of pleading

---

[1] So Brevint: "The Holy Communion is a *Sacramental Passion*;" or, as S. Paul says (1 *Cor.* xi. 26), a "*shewing the Lord's death.*"

and presentation, that Sacrifice of which the Eucharist is the counterpart on earth.

394. The Blessing is given not from the centre of the Altar, but slightly towards the Gospel side, so that the priest, in turning towards the people, should not have his back towards the Blessed Sacrament.

395. *Does the blessing finish the service*

No : the consumption of what remains of the Holy Sacrament, and the ablutions follow.

396. Formerly the Blessed Sacrament was *reserved*, in order to communicate the sick, and others, out of Celebration time. This order was preserved in Edward VI's First Prayer Book, and is still perpetuated in Scotland. The rubric which requires consumption, and which thus *verbally* precludes reservation, was inserted in 1662, not however, as historical evidence abundantly proves, as a bar to reverent reservation, but to make sacrilegious usage of the Sacrament impossible. The authorized Latin Prayer Book of 1560 recognized reservation for the sick as legitimate. [B.]

397. *What are the ablutions ?*

They are small quantities of wine and water which the server pours into the chalice, and which the priest consumes. Some take two ablutions, the first of wine, the second of wine and water mixed. Others add a third of water only, which was the old English custom.

398. *Why does the priest revolve the chalice while the server is pouring in the first ablution ?*

In order to let the wine absorb any drops

that may have adhered to the inside of the chalice.

399. *How is the second ablution made?*

The priest sets the chalice down on the Epistle corner of the altar, and holds the finger and thumb of each hand in the bowl of the chalice, while the server pours first a few drops of wine, and then a larger quantity of water over his fingers into the chalice. The priest having wiped his fingers, then drinks the ablution.

400. *Will you explain these acts?*

They are designed to ensure the *entire consumption* of the Sacred Species, this being essential to the integrity of the Sacrifice (compare *Exod.* xxix. 33);[1] and also to prevent any profane treatment of the Holy Mysteries. Wine is used because it more readily draws to itself anything that remains of the Sacrament of the Blood; water is afterwards added to neutralize the species of wine, whence a considerable quantity is added. Lastly, the second ablution is poured over the priest's fingers, in order that, if any fragment or crumb of the Bread of Life adhere to them, it may be consumed when the priest drinks the ablution. For the same reason,

---

[1] The Holy Eucharist corresponds not only to the Jewish Passover, and to the various forms of Sacrifice, but also to the Showbread; hence, as in the case of reservation, the consumption *need* not take place at the actual time of the Celebration.

before the first ablution, he carefully consumes what remains on the paten, and wipes it with his thumb over the chalice.

401. According to all ancient rites, Eastern and Western, the Ablutions should immediately follow the Communion of priests and people. Liturgically, this is undoubtedly the right place for the ceremony; consumption after the Blessing involves a second Communion at the same Celebration, an obvious irregularity. [B.]

402. *What takes place after the ablutions ?*

The priest returns to the midst of the altar, folds the corporal and other linen; and placing the paten on the chalice, covers all with the silken veil. Then, having bowed before the altar, he returns to the vestry, preceded by the server, who, having assisted him to unvest, re-enters the chancel, extinguishes the altar-lights, and brings the cruets, etc., from the credence-table.

403. *Does the priest always take the ablutions ?*

If he is going to celebrate again that morning, he does not; but putting them into some fitting vessel, he reserves them till the end of the second service, when he partakes of both together.

404. *Why is this ?*

In order that he should not break his fast.

405. *Why ought we to communicate fasting ?*

From motives of reverence. So Bishop

Taylor says: "To him that would honour the Sacrament of Christ's Body and Blood, let it be the *first* Food he eats, the *first* Beverage he drinks."[1] It is a custom of such antiquity and of so universal observance, that S. Chrysostom, when accused of having administered the Eucharist to those who had broken their fast, said: "If I have done such a thing, may my name be blotted out from the roll of bishops!"

406. Fasting Communion was always observed in the Church of England from the earliest times. It is enforced by many Canons, among others the 36th Canon of King Edgar, A.D. 960.

407. *Nevertheless, did not our Lord institute the Holy Eucharist "after Supper"?*

He did so, and some hold that the custom continued till S. Paul, in consequence of the sacrilegious abuses that obtained in the Corinthian Church, commanded early (and fasting) Celebrations, amongst other things which he "set in order" when he came (1 *Cor.* xi. 18-34); a belief that the *antiquity* and *universality* of the practice certainly favour. Besides which, the original institution of the Eucharist was an altogether *exceptional* case; for in it, as Bishop Taylor notes, our Lord made use of the supper *that was wont to follow the* Pascal celebration, to consecrate it to an excellent mystery.

---

[1] So Bishop Sparrow ("Rationale," Oxford ed., p. 216), "This Sacrament is to be received fasting."

408. But it must not be forgotten that, in accordance with the ceremonial observances of the time, our Lord and His Apostles probably came fasting to the celebration of the Paschal Supper. S. Augustine ascribes the institution of the fast before Communion to the Holy Ghost, through the Apostles. Fasting Communion, as the normal rule, is as universally acknowledged in the East as in the West. [B.]

409. *Can the same clergyman then celebrate twice in the day?*

In cases of grave necessity, and on Christmas Day (when, on account of the solemnity, it is a Catholic custom to sing *three* solemn celebrations—one at midnight, when Christ was born; one at dawn, in honour of Him Who that day rose, the "Day-spring from on high;" and one at the usual hour). Otherwise, the same priest should not celebrate more than once. The Excerpts of S. Egbert assign the symbolic reason of this rule, as of the corresponding one, which forbids reception more than once in the same day:[1] "Because Christ suffered but *once*, and redeemed the whole world."

---

[1] Except of course in the case of a priest saying a second Mass; for his reception is essential to the Sacrifice.

SECTION XI

HIGH OR SOLEMN CELEBRATION

410. High Celebration is merely a solemn offering of the Eucharistic Sacrifice with the *full* adjuncts of ritual and music. Ceremonies not described in this Section will therefore be found in the preceding. (Pages 86 to 144.)

411. For an explanation of the vestments of the celebrant and his assistants, and of the choir, see Section III (pp. 18-32), especially paragraphs 75-97.

412. *What is the Introit?*

One or more verses (mostly from the Psalms), sung at the entrance (*ad introitum*) of the clergy into the sanctuary. It consists of two parts—the *Antiphon* or *Anthem*, and the *Psalm*. Sometimes (but improperly) a Hymn is sung in place of the Introit.[1]

413. *Why is the Introit sung?*

As an act of preparation for the Service which follows. So the Psalmist advises: "Let us come before His presence with thanksgiving, and show ourselves glad in Him *with Psalms*" (*Ps.* xcv. 2).

---

[1] A hymn frequently *precedes* the Introit, which should commence as the clergy, having paused in silent prayer before the entrance to the sanctuary, ascend to the altar.

414. The Introit, like the Collect, Epistle, and Gospel, varies with the season. The *Antiphon* is sung in one of the fourteen modes entire before and after the *Psalm* which follows to the corresponding Tone. The *Gloria Patri* is always added, except in funeral Celebrations, and from the fifth Sunday in Lent till Easter. According to old English use, the Antiphon is repeated *thrice* on Sundays and Festivals which have rulers of the choir: at the beginning, and before and after the *Gloria* of the Psalm.

415. *The clergy having silently prayed at the entrance of the sanctuary, ascend the steps of the altar, the deacon to the right of the priest, the subdeacon to his left: the deacon then receives the censer [1] from the thurifer, and presents it to the priest, who incenses the altar in the midst and on each side. Then the deacon censes the priest. Please to explain these ceremonies.*

The deacon ascends to the priest's right, because he is to minister to him; the subdeacon, as the inferior minister, to his left. The custom of using incense at the Eucharist is of very ancient date. It is mentioned in all the oldest Liturgies. The Jews were accustomed to accompany their sacrifices with offerings of incense. Thus Moses says concerning Levi (*Deut.* xxxiii. 10): "They shall put incense before Thee, and whole burnt-sacrifice upon Thine altar." So again Abijah (*2 Chron.* xiii. 10): "The priests ... the sons of Aaron ... burnt unto the Lord every morning and every evening burnt-sacrifices

---

[1] For a description of the censer see paragraph 48.

HIGH OR SOLEMN CELEBRATION 147

and sweet incense." And David prays (*Ps.* cxli. 2): "Let my prayer be set forth before Thee as the incense, and the lifting up of my hands as the evening sacrifice." And Malachi, the last of the prophets, foretelling the days of the Gentile Church, says (ch. i. 11): "In every place incense shall be offered unto My Name, and a Pure Offering." Its use in the *beginning* of the service is also of very ancient date. It is probably here introduced to show that the Church is now beginning her great act of intercession (of which incense is the type; see *Rev.* iii. 5).

416. Before putting it into the censer the priest blesses the incense with these words, "By Him may this incense be blessed in whose honour it shall be burned, in the Name, etc." This is done to set it apart for use in the service of God. (See Section IV.)

For an explanation of the incensing of the altar and of the celebrant, see paragraphs 236, 237.

417. *Why does the deacon hand the censer to the celebrant?*

Because it is his special place to minister to the priest.

418. *I observe that the musical notation to the Kyrie, or response to the Commandments, very frequently varies at the fourth, and again at the seventh response. Can you assign a reason?*

Formerly the *Kyrie Eleison*, or "Lord, have mercy upon us," was repeated *thrice* to God the Father—"*Lord*, have mercy"; *thrice* to God the Son—"*Christ*, have mercy"; and *thrice* to God the Holy Ghost—"*Lord*, have mercy." A separate musical rendering was assigned to each set of *Kyries*.[1] Its use now may serve to remind us that in thought, word, and deed we sin against each Person of the Blessed Trinity, and so should cry aloud for mercy and pardon. (See par. 289.)

419. *Why do the deacon and subdeacon and the other ministers stand during most of the Service?*

Because they are more directly engaged in offering the Sacrifice with the priest.

420. It was a very ancient custom in the Church to set aside *kneeling* entirely in the Easter season, i.e. from Easter to Trinity Sunday, as inconsistent with the spiritual joy which should then fill our hearts. It is customary, in some churches, for the choir to stand throughout the service at this season (except when the priest kneels or genuflects, when they do the same).

421. The deacon stands on the step immediately below the platform of the altar; the subdeacon on the step below that; the other ministers (i.e. the thurifer and acolytes) on the floor of the sanctuary, to mark the different degrees of dignity in the office of each. At the Creed, and again at the *Gloria in Excelsis*,

---

[1] The custom of singing the nine Kyries to ancient or modern music *in substitution* for the Introit is an unliturgical abuse; though there is no reason against singing them immediately *after* the Introit. [B.]

when the priest intones the first few words, the deacon and subdeacon stand in a line behind him on their respective steps; and then as the choir take up the words they ascend, the deacon to the right, the subdeacon to the left of the priest, and stand on the platform of the altar till the Creed or *Gloria* is finished. The same is done at the *Sanctus*. The sacred ministers at these times ascend to the level of the altar, in token that in these parts priest and people are joining with one heart and one voice; they do not ascend till the priest has intoned the initial clause, in acknowledgement that the pastor should be a pattern to his flock, going before and leading them in praise and prayer.

422. *Why does the subdeacon read the Epistle?*

As the inferior minister, it being reserved to the deacon to announce the Holy Gospel.

423. The Epistle and Gospel are *sung* to "a modest and distinct song," in token of the joy with which we should receive the message of God. The Epistle, as the inferior, has the simpler notation, being recited on one note throughout, except an inflexion when an interrogation occurs, and one at the end. The Gospel admits of rather more inflexions. Both these chants are of great antiquity, being derived from the *recitative* of the Greek Drama. The Jews had a solemn chant in their religious offices.

424. It is customary in some places, for the sake of greater solemnity, for the choir to sing

a hymn called the *Sequence*, because it follows (*sequitur*) the Gradual.

425. According to old English use the Sequence was confined to *festivals*, and was not an ordinary Sunday feature, except in Advent or Easter-tide. It was always preceded by a short anthem, called the *Gradual*, to which generally "Alleluia" was added; but in penitential seasons, in place of "Alleluia" several verses, mostly from the Psalms, were added to the Gradual. These were called the *Tract*, from being drawn out (*tractus*) to a mournful cadence. The habit of singing between the Epistle and Gospel is of some antiquity. The Greeks call the anthem here introduced *Prokeimenon*, or "preceding," because it comes before the Gospel.

426. The "Alleluia" (or the Sequence, if there be one) is finished with a *Pneuma*, for reasons given in paragraph 219.

427. Does not the subdeacon in some churches here "prepare" the oblations at the credence?

Yes; where the old English use is followed. While the deacon is preparing to cense the altar before the reading of the Gospel, he goes to the credence, and first places upon the paten the priest's bread, and sufficient for the communicants; and then, in like manner, after begging the priest's benediction on the water (see par. 306), pours into the chalice a sufficient quantity of wine, adding a few drops of the water.

In the Roman rite the breads are placed on the paten, and the chalice is "prepared" at the offertory. (See par. 433.)

HIGH OR SOLEMN CELEBRATION

428. *Why is the Gospel ushered in with the offering of incense?*

The reading of the Gospel is the principal feature of the introductory part of the Eucharistic service, and has ever been accompanied by marks of particular solemnity. S. Jerome testifies to the use of *lights* at the Gospel, as already mentioned (par. 239). The deacon, according to old English usage, receives the censer from the thurifer, and incenses the altar in the midst, as it were asking that the ministry he is about to perform may ascend as the incense in the sight of God. Then, preceded by the thurifer with smoking censer, and by the taper-bearers, he goes to the appointed place, and facing the north, sings the Gospel. This triumphal procession of the deacon signifies the progress of the Gospel of Christ by the ministry of preaching. " Their sound is gone out into all lands, and their words unto the ends of the earth." The *incense* going before proclaims that the preaching of the glad tidings should be accompanied by the odour of good works; as the Apostle says, "We are unto God a sweet savour of Christ" (2 *Cor.* ii. 15); the *lights*, that before the Gospel darkness and the powers of darkness are chased away.

429. In some churches the deacon does not incense the altar, but on arriving at the lectern, where he is to read the Gospel, incenses the book thrice, in token that the odour of virtue proceeds from the Gospel,

as well as for a mark of respect. When the Gospel is over, he incenses the priest. (See paragraphs 237–39.)

430. After the Creed the celebrant (if it be Sunday) announces any festival or fasting days that may happen during the following week, and in parish churches reads the banns of marriage. He here also reads the names of those on whose behalf the prayers of the congregation are desired; and gives notice of confirmations or ordination to be held by the bishop. These notices are given here rather than at Matins, because the Church contemplates the presence of *all* her children at the Eucharistic Sacrifice. Then, if he is to preach, he lays aside his upper garment, or chasuble, and preaches either from the pulpit or from the altar-steps in his alb. He removes his chasuble because the sermon is not *directly* a part of the Sacrifice; retaining his alb, as well to avoid the unseemliness of changing it in the middle of the service, as to mark the distinction between the sermon in the liturgy—which is, as it were, a continuation of the Gospel and Creed—and an ordinary sermon apart from liturgical services. For the same reason the deacon or subdeacon lays aside his dalmatic or tunic, if he is to preach.[1] The priest lays his chasuble *on the altar*, because it is the sacrificial vestment; the

---

[1] And the thurifer and taper-bearers deposit their lights and censer in the vestry.

deacon or subdeacon place their vestments *on the sedilia.*

431. The celebrant, deacon, and subdeacon sit in the sedilia, each one in his appointed place, during the sermon. (See par. 27.) No other clergy, nor any of the inferior ministers, occupy these seats. The acolytes raise the vestments of the priest and sacred ministers when they sit down, to prevent their being injured.

432. *Why do the Choir sing at the Offertory?*

As a mark of joy. So we read in the Book of Chronicles (2 *Chron.* xxix. 27): "When the burnt-offering began, the song of the Lord began also, with the trumpets, and with the instruments ordained by David, King of Israel."

433. *I suppose it is in the same spirit that the third offering of incense here takes place?*

Yes; while the choir is singing the Offertory sentences, the deacon and subdeacon go to the Epistle side of the altar, and if the oblations have been already prepared (see par. 427), the paten and chalice are handed up from the credence by the acolyte to the subdeacon, who delivers them to the deacon, and the deacon to the priest. But if they have to be here prepared, according to the present Latin rite, the subdeacon, having brought up the sacred vessels from the credence, they are there ministered to the priest; the deacon, as the higher minister, serving with the wine, the subdeacon with the water. The priest having made the oblation, as described in paragraph 310, receives the censer from the deacon, and censes the oblations; then the deacon censes the priest, and an acolyte censes the choir, while the priest goes to the Epistle corner for the lavabo.

434. According to the Latin rite, the priest, after having incensed the oblations, proceeds to incense the altar-cross, and then the altar itself, first on the Epistle and then on the Gospel side. The deacon, having incensed the celebrant, goes to incense the choir, and on his return censes the subdeacon, and is himself censed by the thurifer. (For the incensing of the choir see paragraph 237.)

435. At the Confession the deacon and subdeacon, with the other ministers, *kneel*, unless the subdeacon says the Confession, in which case the deacon continues *standing*, as in either case does the celebrant. Kneeling is the sign of humiliation and contrition, and is therefore the attitude of the minister who says the Confession "in the name of" the people, as also of the people themselves, and therefore of the inferior ministers and choir. The celebrant *stands*, because though having need to confess his sins no less than the people, he is here acting *ministerially*. He bows his head and joins his hands, however, in token that he joins *in spirit*, though by his office debarred from joining in act, in the confession of his flock.

436. The direction, "Then shall the priest *stand* up and pronounce the Absolution," supposes him to have

said the Confession in the absence of ministers; in which case he kneels. In practice, however, many celebrants *kneel*, even when the deacon, or some other minister, says the Confession.

437. It is a custom to *chant* the Confession on Maundy Thursday, and when the celebrant is a bishop; at other times it is monotoned. If a bishop is present in choir, or in the sanctuary, he gives the Absolution from his place; but *not* if he is in the body of the church. The same is observed at the Benediction. The reason of this is that " the less is blessed of the greater " (*Heb.* vii. 7). But those in choir, as *leading* divine worship, are *on the particular occasion* greater than those of whatever rank in the body of the church; wherefore neither benedictions or absolutions are given from the latter place. The chancel also represents heaven, from whence the blessing of God is shed on His people.

438. *Why does the priest chant the Preface, and the sentences that precede it?*

For the sake of solemnity. This chant, which is more elaborate than that used at the Gospel, is of great antiquity.

439. According to the ceremonial used in some places towards the end of the Preface, one of the acolytes kindles the two tall candles which stand before the altar, first on the Gospel side, afterwards that on the Epistle side. This is in honour of the *Sanctus*, which is about to commence, and of the canon, which it ushers in. (See par. 335.)

440. *What is the Benedictus?*

It is a short anthem added to the *Sanctus* in solemn celebrations. It is called the *Benedictus* (or more properly, to distinguish it from the song of Zacharias, *Benedictus qui venit*) from the first words of the Latin version. It runs: "Blessed is He that cometh in the Name of the Lord. Hosanna in the highest." It is generally sung after the priest has recited in a low voice the Prayer of Humble Access, and has reference to the *coming* of our Lord, which is about to take place through the Consecration.

441. While it is being sung the taper-bearers again fetch their candles as at the Gospel, and kneel on the floor of the sanctuary, opposite the Gospel and Epistle sides of the altar. Lights are here employed in honour of our Lord's mystic presence, now about to be vouchsafed. In the East lamps were borne before the bridegroom at weddings (see *S. Matt.* xxv. 1), and in the Temple service lamps were lit before the Lord (*Exod.* xl. 25). And our Blessed Lord counsels His disciples to let their loins be girded and their lights burning, and to be like men that wait for their lord when he will return from the wedding (*S. Luke* xii. 35, 36).

442. Incense is used at the consecration for the same reason; and in the spirit of the wise men, who offered to the newborn Saviour " gold, *frankincense*, and myrrh " (*S. Matt.* ii. 11).

443. *Why does the deacon at the beginning of the Canon ascend to the priest's left?*

In case he has to turn over the pages of the book. Shortly before the actual words of consecration he ascends to the right of the priest, and kneels down till after the consecration of the bread. He then rises and removes the pall from the chalice, and then kneels till after the consecration of the chalice. The subdeacon kneels when the deacon first does, but does not rise till after the second consecration.

444. *What is the Agnus Dei?*

It is an anthem sung by the choir during the Communion of the priest; and is a prayer to our Lord now present on the altar, "the Lamb as it had been slain" (*Rev.* v. 6). The choir sing thrice: "O Lamb of God, that takest away the sins of the world," adding twice "have mercy upon us," and the third time, "Grant us Thy peace." The threefold repetition is considered to have reference to the Holy Trinity, to the God Who "sent forth the Lamb, the ruler of the earth" (*Isa.* xvi. 1).[1]

445. It is said that the responsory clauses were originally the same all three times, but that the Prayer for Peace was added as persecution (and the spirit of division) abounded, in order to crave peace and unity for the Church. It is therefore a fitting occasion to pray for that true "peace" of the Church which can alone take place when the scattered portions are reunited in one visible unity: when the "multitude of them that believe" shall be once more "of one heart and of one soul," as at the first (*Acts* iv. 32).

446. Both the *Benedictus* before consecration, and the *Agnus Dei* after, were continued in Edward VI's First Liturgy; and so were among the things afterwards abandoned rather by the "curiosity of the minister and mistakers, than of any other worthy cause."

---

[1] The Vulgate or Latin version of this passage reads: "Send, O Lord, the Lamb, the Ruler of the earth, from Sela (or the rock) to the wilderness," and is referred by mystical writers to the sending forth of our Lord by the Father into the "wilderness" of the world to accomplish our salvation.

447. During the Communion of the people (see par. 375–81) it is customary for the organist to play soft strains of music, both to fill up the pause and as an act of homage by the exercise of his art to our Lord. Thus David played on the harp before King Saul (1 *Sam.* xvi. 23); and " on all manner of instruments before the Lord," when he brought the ark up to Jerusalem (2 *Sam.* vi. 5).

448. *Why is the Lord's Prayer sung to a solemn chant after the Communion of the people?*

Because it is here employed *festally*, as an act of thanksgiving. The priest chants the first words, and the choir take it up, and continue it to the end, as is done in the Creed, *Sanctus*, and *Gloria in Excelsis*.

449. At the ablutions the subdeacon ministers to the priest while the deacon is engaged in folding up the corporals, etc.; or else both deacon and subdeacon assist at the ablutions— the former with the wine, the latter with the water, as at the oblations. (See par. 433.)

450. After the ablutions, and when the chalice is duly covered with its veil as at the first, the choir and ministers return *in order* into the vestry; first the choir two and two, then the lay clerks, then the clergy in choir, then the ministers, deacon, and subdeacon, and lastly the celebrant. Occasionally the choir sings the *Nunc Dimittis* during the passage back into the vestry. The candles are then extinguished by an acolyte, as at a Low Celebration.

SECTION XII

FUNERAL AND MORTUARY CELEBRATIONS

451. *Why is the Holy Eucharist celebrated at funerals?*

To show that the deceased departed hence in the Communion of the Church, and also to beg for him peace and rest in the habitations of light.

452. *Is it an ancient custom to offer the Eucharist for the departed?*

Yes; the earliest liturgies contain commemorations of and petitions for the dead, and ancient writers, e.g. Tertullian (*De Coron. Mil.* c. 3), SS. Chrysostom (*Hom. on Phil.* i. 24), Augustus (*Eucheir.*), and other ancient writers testify to its being offered at stated times for the Dead specially.

453. *What are these stated times?*

They are chiefly the day of burial, and the anniversary of departure. The latter was called by our forefathers the *Year's-mind* or *Twelve-month's-mind*.

454. The *Month's-mind* was a solemn commemoration of a departed person during the month following his decease, more especially the third, seventh, and thirtieth

days. Mortuary celebrations were also offered at any other time (except on Good Friday), according to the bequests of the deceased or the piety and care of their surviving relatives.

455. For *All Souls' Day*, or the commemoration of all the faithful departed, see below, par. 466.

456. *Do mortuary celebrations differ in ceremonial from ordinary celebrations?*

Yes; they have a liturgical colour proper to themselves; they have also a proper Introit (Collect, Epistle, and Gospel[1]); the order of incensing and the form of the *Agnus Dei* also vary, with a few other peculiarities.

457. *What is the liturgical colour assigned to mortuary celebrations?*

Black, to signify, by its mournful hue, not so much the grief of the survivors as the truth that death came into the world by *sin*; that all have fallen and come short of the goodness of God, and stand in need of His pardon.

458. *What is the Introit in these celebrations?*

It is an adaptation of 2 Esdras ii. 34, 35, followed by a verse of the 65th Psalm, the *Gloria* (as a sign of joy) being omitted; and runs as follows: "Grant them, O Lord, eternal rest, and let light perpetual shine upon them. Thou, O God, art praised in Sion, and unto

---

[1] These are given in Edward's first book, and in the Latin Prayer Book of Elizabeth, but are not contained in the Prayer Book as at present set forth.

FUNERAL AND MORTUARY CELEBRATIONS 161

Thee shall the vow be performed in Jerusalem. Thou that hearest the prayer, unto Thee shall all flesh come."

459. *How does the order of incensation vary?*

The priest does not cense the altar at the Introit, nor does the deacon do so before singing the Gospel, which is sung without the usual accompaniments of lights and incense. At the Offertory he censes the oblations in the usual manner, but the choir is not censed.

460. According to old English use, however, whenever the corpse was present the deacon censed it at the Introit, and again (having previously censed the altar as usual) before singing the Gospel; and lastly, the priest, after censing the oblations, descended and censed the corpse.

461. *Will you explain these variations?*

Incense being a joyful feature is used less sparingly in mortuary celebrations. It is omitted at the Introit and Gospel, because the introductory or *didactic* part of the Liturgy is inapplicable to the departed! and in the latter case because the dead can no longer have the Gospel preached to them, or shape their conduct according to its maxims, but must be judged and rewarded according as they have done so when in the body. For the same reason the acolytes accompany the deacon without their usual lights, but with their hands folded on their breasts.

462. The corpse is censed to show that it was made the temple of the Holy Ghost in Baptism, and that the soul which lately inhabited it departed in communion with the Church, and was partaker of the altar.

463. *What other peculiarity have you to notice?*

The priest does not bless the water as usual before putting it into the chalice.

464. *Why is this?*

The water signifies the Church militant, as the wine does Christ; the water is not therefore blessed, because the service is not offered primarily for the Church's children militant here on earth, but for those who have fought the good fight, and now rest from their labours. The incense, however, is blessed at the Offertory, because it is symbolical of the merits of Christ which are pleaded in this Sacrifice, and because, as such, it is offered to God together with the oblations.

465. *What variation is there in the* Agnus Dei?

In place of the response " Have mercy upon us " is repeated " Grant them rest "; and in place of " Grant us Thy peace " " Grant them rest eternal."

466. *What is the* Dies Irae?

It is a sequence very frequently sung in funeral and other mortuary celebrations. It was composed by Thomas Celano, a Franciscan friar, about the middle of the twelfth century, and is considered the finest hymn extant. It was not admitted as a sequence for the dead for some time (sequences as a joyous feature being considered out of place), nor was it ever enjoined as such in the old English offices, though the printed missals gave it for those priests who might desire to say it. In the present Roman rite its use is compulsory at High Celebrations, on All Souls' Day, and when the corpse is present; at other times it is optional.

SECTION XIII

THE OCCASIONAL SERVICES

467. *Why does the priest use two stoles in administering Baptism, the first violet, the second white?*

As an emblem of the gift of regeneration bestowed therein. For being by nature born in sin, the person baptized is hereby made the child of grace.

468. *Why does he divide the water in the form of a cross at the words "Sanctify this water"?*

Because he here solemnly sets apart the water to its sacramental use. For the same reason the water is let off immediately after the Baptism.

469. A name is given to show that the child is dedicated to the service of Jesus Christ. This is usually the name of one of God's saints, as S. Chrysostom (*Homil.* 21, *in Gen.*) and others remark, in order that the child in after years may be stirred up to imitate the virtues and sanctity of him whose name he bears.

470. The child is baptized with *trine* (i.e. threefold) immersion, or trine affusion, once at

the name of each Person of the Blessed Trinity, to show yet more clearly the truth that he is baptized into the faith of the Three-in-One. In trine *immersion* the child is first immersed with the face towards the north, the second time towards the south, and lastly with his face towards the water, to show that he is translated from the Kingdom of Satan to the Kingdom of Grace.

471. A lighted candle is sometimes given to the child, or to the godfather, as a sign that he must henceforth walk by the light of faith. Formerly he was anointed with *oil*, and then clothed in a white garment called the *chrisom*. Both these customs are of the greatest antiquity, and were continued in Edward VI's First Liturgy.

472. Baptism is wont to be "solemnly" administered on the vigils of Easter and Pentecost. The Gospel is *chanted* as in a Solemn Celebration. The reason is because these were the two great times for baptizing converts in the Primitive Church.

473. *Why is a person, about whose having been previously baptized there is any doubt, only baptized "conditionally"?*

Because it is not lawful to confer the Sacrament of Baptism *twice*. The same is the case with Confirmation and Holy Orders. The reason is, that these three Ordinances confer a *lasting mark*, or "character"; and to repeat them is therefore sacrilege.

474. The Forms of Ordering of Deacons and of Priests, and of Consecrating of Bishops, are only

successive *stages* in the single rite of "Holy Orders."[1] Thus a bishop translated to a fresh see, even though that see be an *arch*bishopric, is not *reconsecrated*. Similarly a Roman or Greek priest conforming to the English Church receives no fresh ordination. A Dissenting minister has to be ordained before he can officiate as deacon or priest, because he is not in Holy Orders, which require episcopal laying on of hands.

475. *Why are marriages performed with white vestments ?*

Because matrimony is a "mystery" (*Eph.* v. 32) or sacramental rite, setting forth the spiritual marriage or unity between Christ and His Church. (See *Rev.* xix. 7, 8.)

476. *Why is the office begun in "the body of the church," and afterwards continued before the altar ?*

Because it consists of two distinct parts— the betrothal, and the nuptial benediction. The latter, as the sacramental part, is alone performed in the sanctuary.

477. Formerly the betrothal and the nuptial benediction took place on different occasions.

478. At the "plighting of the troth" the woman has her hand uncovered if she have not been previously married, but covered if she be a widow. This is done to mark the distinction

---

[1] This is why the sacred ministers at a High Celebration wear the *habits* of a deacon or a subdeacon, *even though they may be in priest's orders*. Every priest is also a deacon, every bishop is also a priest; the greater orders contain in them the less.

which from the earliest times the Church has made between *first* and *second* marriages, in order to set forth the *unity* of that which earthly espousals signify—the Marriage of the Lamb.

479. Marriage in the first instance hath been *instituted* by God; second marriages are *permitted* (S. Ambrose).[1] For the same reason formerly the nuptial benediction was not given in second marriages, and passages alluding to the union betwixt Christ and His Church were omitted.

480. It is an old custom for the man to place the ring first on the *thumb* of the bride, then her *second* finger, and then on her *third*, at the name of each Person of the Holy Trinity, "leaving it," as the rubric directs, on her fourth finger at the word Amen; thus signifying by action not less than by word that he was undertaking the duties of the married state "in the Name of the Father, of the Son, and of the Holy Ghost." The reason assigned for the fourth finger being appointed as the final resting-place of the wedding ring is singular —"because on that finger there is a certain vein which proceeds to the heart." The *left* hand was appointed, probably, because the virgins espoused to Christ wore the ring of their celestial nuptials on the *right* hand. Ritualists see in the ring a type of the *eternal* union between Christ and His Spouse the Church; and of the consequent indissoluble nature of the marriage-tie; and in the gold, of which it is generally composed, a symbol of the pure love which subsists between them (*Eph.* v. 25; *Cant.* ii. 16), and which should find its counterpart in earthly marriages.

481. The priest was in some places accustomed to entwine the ends of his stole round the joined hands of

---

[1] "Primae nuptiae a Domino sunt constitutae; secundae vero permissae. Primae nuptiae sub omni benedictione celebrantur: secundae vero carent omni benedictione."

the man and woman, at the words "Those whom God hath joined together," in token of the indissoluble union therein effected.

482. At the Celebration which follows (*Missa Sponsalium*) the bride and bridegroom kneel at the south side of the church, between the choir and the sanctuary; and there is a special introit and sequence, because the Holy Eucharist is specially offered to implore grace and benediction on the newly-married couple.

483. In the Latin Prayer Book of Queen Elizabeth (1560), after the last blessing there follows the rubric: "Deinde sequetur communio," with this note at the end of the service, "Observandum, quod desponsati debeant participes fieri mensae Domini"; from which it appears that the Church intended a celebration to take place even if the newly-married, from any cause, declined to communicate.

484. Marriages are forbidden to be solemnized, by precept of the Church, at certain seasons; viz. from Advent to the Octave of the Epiphany;[1] from Septuagesima to the Octave of Easter; and from Rogation Sunday to the Octave of Pentecost. The reason is, because at these times the Church is either calling us to penitential exercises, with which a joyful solemnity would be out of place, or is celebrating one of the three great festivals of our Lord, and so

---

[1] Custom, however, sanctioned marriages on the *Octave-day itself* of the Epiphany, and on Trinity Sunday; in the first case probably on account of the few days that frequently intervened before Septuagesima; in the second, because it is not so much the Octave of Pentecost as the beginning of a new season.

would bid us avoid distraction, in order to "keep a solemn feast unto the Lord" (*Deut.* xvi. 15; see also *Exod.* xxiii. 14).

485. In the Visitation of the Sick, and in hearing confessions, the priest wears a surplice —the *ministerial*, as opposed to the *sacrificial* or choral garb—and a stole of *violet* colour, because of the penitential aspect of these ordinances. In privately celebrating for the Communion of the Sick the priest wears the Eucharistic vestments; violet should be the colour employed.

486. The First Prayer Book of Edward VI directed the priest to "anoint" the sick person "upon the forehead or breast, making the sign of the Cross," if he desired to be anointed. This anointing of the sick is of the greatest antiquity, and indeed is derived from the express command of S. James (ch. v. 14): "Is any sick among you? let him call for the elders of the Church; and let them pray over him, *anointing him with oil* in the Name of the Lord."

487. In the Eastern Church the anointing of the sick is called the "Mystery," or Sacrament, "of the Prayer Oil." It, together with the confession to which the sick man is to be "moved," gives the sacramental character to the Visitation of the Sick.[1] "If the sick layman," says Archbishop Ælfric, "desire to receive unction, let him then confess, and forgive every grudge, before the unction."

---

[1] The homilies mention "Matrimony," "Absolution," "Order," "Confirmation," and "*Visitation of the Sick*" as "Sacraments," though distinguishing them from the "two great Sacraments of the Gospel."

488. The Holy Communion, when administered to the sick man at the point of death, is called the *Viaticum*, i.e. the "provision for the way." So important has the Church ever considered "the last Sacrament," that the *Viaticum* was not to be denied to the greatest sinners, if they showed signs of repentance. The 13th canon of the Council of Nice ordered all men to receive the *Viaticum*. For the same reason the Church has seen fit to suspend the otherwise universal custom of *communicating fasting* (see pars. 405–8), when the Blessed Sacrament is received by way of *Viaticum*.

489. Formerly in many places the priest was wont to give the *Viaticum* with a different form: "Receive the *Viaticum* of the Body of our Lord Jesus Christ, and may It preserve thy body and soul," etc. And before Its reception the priest exhorted the sick man to "wash himself with the tears of contrition, that he might be worthy to eat the Bread of Life, even the Sacrament of the Body of Christ, which shall be to thee in this way, in which thou art setting forth, strength and support: so shalt thou go by God's grace, in the strength of this meat, even to the Mount of God."

490. If the sick person be unable to retain the sacred species in his stomach (in which case of course it would be the grossest profanity to communicate him), or if a priest cannot be had in time, the Rubric directs him to make an Act of Spiritual Communion. (See par. 380.)

491. *Why is mention made of the " priest and clerks" at the beginning of the Burial Service ?*

Because it is the Church's intention that, whenever possible, the bodies of her children should be committed to the earth with the solemnity of a choral service.

492. The "young men" mentioned in the Acts (v. 6, 10) as assisting at the burial of Ananias and Sapphira have been supposed to be an order of inferior ministers in the Apostolic Church—whether subdeacons or acolytes—to whom this office was appointed. S. Ignatius, in saluting the different orders and degrees in the Church of Antioch, salutes "τοὺς κοπιῶντας—the labourers," which some interpret the acolytes; others those who had the care of burying the dead. The Church has ever included "burying the dead" (i.e. assisting at their obsequies) among the "Works of Mercy."

493. The Burial Service consists of three parts: the "Office," consisting of the anthems and psalms, with the lesson; the "Celebration," or Requiem Mass; and the "Deposition," or burial proper. The singing of the Psalms before a funeral in the presence of the corpse is of old institution. "If we are occupied with the funeral solemnities of the departed," says S. Chrysostom, "David is first, last, and midst." Sometimes the *whole Psalter* was so recited; but more ordinarily, the body having been brought into church overnight, a service, called the "Vigils of the Dead," consisting of Evensong, followed by Matins and Lauds, was sung.

494. *Incense* is used at funerals in recognition of the Communion of Saints—the truth, that is, that the departed are not severed from the Church on earth, but that they still hold communion with her, being the objects of her *intercession*

(of which incense is the type), and also interceding for her. For the same reason the body is incensed, as also to show our reverence for that which was the temple of the Holy Ghost (1 *Cor.* vi. 19); which was illuminated and regenerated in Holy Baptism, was fed on Christ in the Eucharist, and which some day will be raised again, being awakened (as our trust is) to a joyful resurrection.

495. In funeral processions *the cross* is carried before, to show that, as the deceased was signed with the cross in Baptism, in token that he should not be ashamed to confess the faith of Christ crucified, and to fight under His banner, so he has departed in the same faith. For a similar reason the sacred sign is also marked on the funeral pall.

496. *The tapers* used in funeral solemnities signify that "the souls of the departed are not put out, but having walked here as children of light, are now gone to walk before God in the light of the living." They tell of *immortality*, and of the final triumph over the grave, when death shall be swallowed up in victory.

497. It is a vexed question among ritualists as to the proper *colour* to be employed in funeral obsequies. All are agreed that all unnecessary gloominess should be avoided; and that the arrangements should be such as speak of Christian hope, and not of the despair of sorrow as they that have no hope. For this end the pall is usually of a more cheerful hue than black, generally *violet* trimmed with *red* (or with white for

young unmarried persons); and so we find the old English use employing a variety of colours for the pall. But in the funeral celebration, when we pray God to "remember not the offences" of the departed, it is usual to employ *black* vestments, remembering that death came into the world by *sin*. Some, however, for the reasons stated above, would employ *violet* even in the Eucharistic vestments.

498. At the funerals of *infants*, that is of children dying under and up to seven years of age, white is employed both in the pall and in the vestments of the clergy, because of those alone we can be *sure* that they sleep in Jesus, and so can rejoice without any admixture of mournful sentiment. "It is CERTAIN by God's word, that children, which are baptized, dying before they commit actual sin, are undoubtedly saved." For the same reason the bell is not tolled, and in many places a separate part of the cemetery or churchyard is reserved for the infants. It is usual to place on such a crown of flowers, "as a sign of the integrity and chastity of their flesh." The processional cross is borne without the staff, as signifying that, though signed with the sign of the cross, and made partakers of the benefits of Christ's Passion, they were not required to carry their cross after Him.

499. Clergy and Sisters are buried in the habits of their Order, because having entered the ecclesiastical or religious *state*, they will be judged at the last day as ecclesiastics or religious. It is not unusual for Sisters and virgins espoused to Christ to be buried with white palls, trimmed with black or violet; but white vestments are not used by the officiants, because, though their state is one of purity and integrity, they stand in need of the prayers and suffrages of the faithful, since in many things we offend all.

500. In the "Churching of Women" the priest uses a *white* stole, because it is a service

of thanksgiving. For the same reason is the "decent apparel" of the woman—that is, according to Catholic custom—a white veil. The service begins at the church door, or at least without the choir, and the priest leads the woman into the chancel—either by the right hand, or by giving her the extremity of his stole—after the Psalm, because child-bearing fell under the curse of sin (*Gen.* iii. 16), and this service is designed to show that the curse pronounced upon Eve has been done away by the grace of Christ, Who has instituted matrimony "for the procreation of children to be brought up in the fear and admonition of the Lord, and to the praise of His Holy Name."

501. The woman maketh her accustomed offering in token of thanksgiving, according to the commandment of the Lord: "Thou shalt not appear before the Lord *empty*: every man shall give as he is able, according to the blessing of the Lord thy God, which He hath given thee" (*Deut.* xvi. 16, 17).

SECTION XIV

CEREMONIES PECULIAR TO CERTAIN SEASONS

502. Why does the Christian year begin with the first Vespers of Advent Sunday?

Because the Church "does not number her days or measure her seasons so much by the motion of the sun as by the course of her Saviour; beginning and pursuing her year with Him Who, being the true 'Sun of Righteousness,' began as at this time to rise upon the world, and as the 'Day-Star' on high to enlighten them that sit in spiritual darkness."

503. For the same reason the Church begins her commemorations of the saints with the Feast of S. Andrew (November 30th), he being the first Apostle who received our Lord's call—whence the Greeks style him the *Protoclete*, or "first called"; and Advent Sunday is always the Sunday *nearest* to this festival, whether before or after, or on the day itself.

504. Advent Sunday, as the head of the sacred season of preparation for the Christmas festival, is reckoned as a Sunday of the first or highest class, and always supersedes any festival that may fall on the same day. The other Sundays in Advent are of the second class, and take precedence of all but the highest feasts, because the Church is unwilling to turn from the contemplation of our Lord's approach-

ing Advent in the flesh, which she is about to celebrate at Christmas, and of His second coming, to which she looks, except for grave cause. For the same reason the weekdays in Advent are "Greater Ferias," and take precedence of the *lower class* feasts.

505. Exactly the same rule holds good with regard to *Lent*. The first Sunday (on which the season formerly began) is reckoned as a Sunday of the first class, for the same cause as Advent Sunday is; the three following Sundays are of the second class, the weekdays "Greater Ferias." The two last Sundays, as appertaining to *Passiontide*, are also of the first class; the weekdays "Greater Ferias," except the three days before Easter, which are "Double" Solemnities of the first class; though, from their peculiar character, lacking first Vespers. *Ash Wednesday* is a "Greater Feria"; but, on account of its solemnity as the "head of the fast," takes precedence even of the highest feasts. Septuagesima and the two following Sundays (which form a kind of preparation for Lent) are of the second rank.

506. In Advent and Lent the deacon and subdeacon lay aside the dalmatic or tunic, as being a *festal* garment, and minister in the *planeta*, or folded chasuble, or in their albs.

507. The *planeta*, or planet (so called because from being folded back it presented the appearance of a star when partially eclipsed), is reckoned a penitential vestment, for which reason the subdeacon removes it when he is about to sing the Epistle, and the deacon does the same when he sings the Gospel. The subdeacon, however, resumes it immediately after the Epistle; but the deacon ministers in the alb till the Post-Communion, when he resumes the planet.

508. The deacon and subdeacon resume the dalmatic and tunic on Christmas Eve, if it fall on Sunday (and

in the Roman rite, though not according to old English use, on the third Sunday in Advent, and the fourth Sunday in Lent also). The reason assigned is that Advent is a time partly of sorrow and partly of joy, and in the lessons for the third Sunday the joyous element predominates (as it does also in the Epistle for the fourth Sunday). On the fourth Sunday in Lent the Church makes a kind of pause in her penitential exercises (whence it was called *Refreshment Sunday*), saying as it were with the Psalmist: "Though I walk in the midst of trouble, yet shalt Thou refresh me" (*Ps.* cxxxviii. 7). Where this custom obtains it was usual to employ purple dalmatics richly embroidered in gold, or to use vestments of a *rose colour*, yet further to symbolize the temporary change from sorrow to joy. "Thou hast put off my sackcloth, and girded me with gladness" (*Ps.* xxx. 12). "The desert shall rejoice and blossom as the rose; it shall blossom abundantly, and rejoice even with joy and singing" (*Isa.* xxxv. 1, 2).

509. The dalmatic and tunic are worn on all festivals when the service is of the festival (i.e. when it is not superseded by the Sunday service), both in Advent and Lent; and on Maundy Thursday—*propter solemnitatem coenae*—because the Church tempers her sorrowful memorial of our Lord's Passion with an element of gladness on account of the Institution of the Holy Eucharist.

510. On the last eight days of Advent, beginning with December 16th, the greater antiphons are sung at Evensong before and after the *Magnificat*. These antiphons were formerly called the O's, as each one began with that word. December 16th is marked in the Calendar "O Sapientia," from the first words of the first of these antiphons: "O Wisdom, which camest forth out of the mouth of the Most High, and reachest from one end to the other, mightily and sweetly ordering all things: come and teach us the way of prudence."

511. *Why is there a celebration at midnight on Christmas Day?*

Because that was the hour in which our Lord was born. It was customary to celebrate *three* High Masses on Christmas Day, the first at midnight, for the reason given above; the second at daybreak, in honour of the Dayspring from on high, Who on this day dawned upon the world; the third at the usual hour after Matins. The *threefold* celebration also was not without reference to the work of the Blessed Trinity in the Incarnation. (See par. 409.)

512. The choir children are accustomed to sing carols during the Christmas season both in church and at the houses of the faithful, in imitation of the angels who at this time sang the first *Gloria in Excelsis*, when they told the " glad tidings " to the shepherds at Bethlehem.

513. Special functions were assigned the *boys* attached to the church at Christmastide, in honour of the childhood of our Blessed Lord. Of this kind was the observance of the *Boy Bishop*, which commenced on the Feast of S. Nicolas (who is accounted the patron saint of children), and ended on that of the Holy Innocents, or Childermas. The choir elected one of their number, who assumed the episcopal dress during this time, and preached a sermon. In choir the boy bishop sang the service, the children occupying the *upper* stalls, the clergy and lay clerks the lower. In this custom (not without a quaint beauty) our forefathers saw an allusion to the childlike spirit inculcated by our Saviour, when He took a little child and

set him in the midst as a model to His disciples and Apostles. The observance has long been obsolete. The custom of constructing a manger or crib in one of the aisles or side-chapels is still continued in some places. Tapers are burned round it in honour of Him Who is the brightness of the morning, and whose light at this time dawned upon the world.

514. The decoration of churches with evergreens in times of festivity is derived from the rites of natural religion. The evergreens remain throughout the Octave of the Epiphany (which is the complement of Christmas), or until Candlemas Day when that feast falls before Septuagesima; in this case the decorations are removed prior to the Vigil.[1] But if they become shabby or faded they should be removed after the Epiphany.

515. *Why are candles distributed on the Purification of the Blessed Virgin?*

In allusion to the words of Symeon at the presentation of our Saviour in the Temple, " To be a *light* to lighten the Gentiles." Hence the popular term "Candlemas Day." The candles are borne in the procession because Christ was *carried* to the Temple; at the Gospel, because it tells of His presentation; and from the consecration to the end of the

---

[1] The *Easter decorations* remain from Easter till the Octave of Corpus Christi; thus including the whole of the Paschal season, the Whitsun and Trinity Octaves, and the Octave commemorating our Lord's mystical Presence in the Eucharist. It will be seldom, however, that they can be maintained in good condition for so long.

service, because He, the true Light, is there present.

516. *Is this custom of any antiquity?*

Yes; the procession with tapers is mentioned by Gelasius, S. Ildefonsus, S. Eligius, S. Sophronius, Patriarch of Jerusalem, S. Cyril of Alexandria, and other fathers in their sermons on this festival. It is probably coeval with the institution of the feast itself.

517. Ælfric, Archbishop of Canterbury, in his homily for this day, tells us that the custom among our Anglo-Saxon forefathers was for each one to bring his candle to his parish church, to be there blessed and then carried in procession: "Be it known to every one that it is appointed in the ecclesiastical observances that we on this day bear our lights to church and let them be there blessed; and that we should go afterwards with the light among God's houses and sing the hymn that is thereto appointed. Though some men cannot sing, they can, nevertheless, bear the light in their hands; for on this day was Christ, the true Light, borne to the temple, Who redeemed us from darkness, and bringeth us to the eternal light." Bede, after speaking of the old heathen lustration ordained by Numa, says: "But this lustration hath the Christian religion well changed, when in the same month, on the day of Blessed Mary, all the people, with the priests and ministers, proceed with the voice of hymnody through the church, and through fitting places of the city, carrying burning tapers in their hands which they receive from the bishop, . . . and this not for the lustration once in five years of an earthly empire, but in perpetual memory of a heavenly kingdom; when, according to the parable of the Wise Virgins, all the elect, with the lamps of good works burning brightly in

their hands, shall go forth to meet their Spouse and King, and shall straightway enter with Him to the banquet of the celestial city." S. Bernard says, "This holy procession was first made by the Virgin Mother, S. Joseph, holy Symeon, and Anna, to be afterwards performed in all places and by every nation, with the exultation of the whole earth to honour this mystery." And he thus describes it: "We go in procession, two by two, carrying candles in our hands, which are lighted, not at a common fire, but a fire first blessed in the church by a bishop. They that go out first return last; and in the way we sing, 'Great is the glory of the Lord.' We go two by two in commendation of charity and a social life; for so our Saviour sent out His disciples. We carry lights in our hands—first, to signify that our light should shine before men; secondly, this we do this day especially in memory of the Wise Virgins (of whom this blessed Virgin is the chief) that went to meet their Lord with their lamps lit and burning. And from this usage and the many lights set up in the church this day it is called Candelaria, or Candlemas. Because our works should be all done in the holy fire of charity; therefore the candles are lit with holy fire. They that go out first return last to teach humility, 'in humility preferring one another.' Because God loveth a cheerful giver, therefore we sing in the way. The procession itself is to teach us that we should stand not idle in the way of life, but proceed from virtue to virtue, not looking back to that which is behind, but reaching forward to that which is before."

518. *What is Septuagesima?*

The third Sunday before Lent. The period between this Sunday and Easter is sometimes called the "greater Lent," and is supposed to refer to the seventy years' captivity of the children of Israel, when they hung their harps by the waters of Babylon, saying, "How shall we sing the Lord's song in a strange land?" Hence the word "Alleluia," which signifies "Praise the Lord," and is a joyful song, is omitted during these seventy days. It was formerly the custom to sing the "Alleluia" many times over in the service just before Septuagesima. This was called the "farewell to Alleluia." The "Alleluiatic sequence," that is, the hymn beginning "The strain upraise of joy and praise, Alleluia," was so employed in Germany, and the hymn "Alleluia, song of sweetness," by the Anglo-Saxon Church, and later in the Diocese of Worcester.[1]

519. Septuagesima is a season of preparation for the Lent feast, whence the Church begins to read in her first lessons the Book of Genesis, which tells of man's fall, to dispose us to repent of and put away that sin by which death and sorrow came into the world.

---

[1] The Church retains the Hebrew words, *Alleluia, Hosanna, Amen*, and the like, rather than their vernacular equivalents, as a sign of her Hebrew origin and in token that the law is summed up in the Gospel. So formerly (and still in the Latin Church) the Greek phrases *Kyrie eleison, Christe eleison, Agios O Theos*, and the like, were employed (according to Martene, in early times the Latin *miserere nobis* was similarly used by the Greeks) as a sign that, whatever be her language, the Church is one. Thus the "Hebrew, Greek, and Latin" (*S. John* xix. 20) were employed by the Liturgies of the Church; and a tradition asserts that on the conversion of the Jews the Church will be visibly one under these threefold aspects—the Hebrew, Greek, and Latin Churches.

CEREMONIES PECULIAR TO SEASONS 183

520. Why is Shrove Tuesday so called?

From an old Saxon word signifying to *confess*. "In the week immediately before Lent every one shall go to his confessor and confess his deeds; and his confessor shall so shrive him as he then may hear by his deeds what he is to do; and he shall command all his parishioners with God's command, that if any of them against any man have any enmity, that he make peace with him; but if any one will not agree to that then he may not shrive him, but then he shall acquaint the bishop that he may turn him to right. . . . Then with minds thus purified let them enter on the tide of the holy fast, and by penance purify themselves against the holy Easter."—*Ecclesiastical Institutes.*[1]

521. What is Ash Wednesday?

The first day of Lent, so called because ashes were wont to be blessed and put upon the foreheads of the people in sign of penitence, the priest as he marked the cross on each one's brow, saying, "Remember, O man, that thou art dust, and unto dust shalt thou return."

522. The six Psalms appointed for Ash Wednesday at Matins and Evensong, with that sung in the Commination Service form the "Seven Penitential Psalms," which were frequently recited during Lent from very early times. The Commination Service is a kind of

---

[1] *Ancient Laws of England*, ed. Thorpe, ii. 433.

memorial of the ancient ceremony of the expulsion by the bishop of notorious sinners from the Church, into which they were not readmitted till Maundy Thursday.

523. The proper hymns for Lent do not begin till the first Vespers of the Sunday, because the previous days are merely supplemental, having been added in order to complete the number of *forty days*, without reckoning in the Sundays, which, as weekly memorials of the Resurrection, are not included in the days of *fasting*. The old English and some other Service books divided Lent into three stages, by the use of a fresh set of hymns at the third as well as the fifth Sunday, in order to show the progression in holiness that should attend our penitential exercises: " They will go from strength to strength " (*Ps.* lxxxiv. 5–7). The three divisions of Lent also typified the three night watches of a beleagured city, Lent representing the time of sorrow and penance, and so of the earthly exile of the Church "going through the vale of misery."

524. Before the first Vespers of the fifth Sunday in Lent, when the Church begins to celebrate the Passion of our Lord (whence this Sunday is called *Passion Sunday*, and the week that follows, " Passion Week "),[1] it is customary to *veil* crosses and pictures throughout the church; they remain covered till the celebration of the Easter festival. Veiling or covering is a sign of mourning (*Isa.* xxv. 7); and in some parts of the church the crosses and

---

[1] The whole fortnight is called *Passiontide* (see par. 138) ; and the last week *Holy Week*, or the " Great Week " ; though colloquially *this* week has come to be called " Passion Week " in England, and in some parts of Germany.

pictures were accordingly veiled throughout Lent. The spirit of the Passiontide veiling seems to be, that the Church would draw off our attention from everything but Him whose suffering she is commemorating, bidding us "consider Him that endured such contradiction of sinners." It is also symbolical of the hiding of our Lord's glory during His earthly life, and especially during His ignominious and bitter Passion.

525. According to the old English uses, the veiling extended from the *first Monday* in Lent to the morning of Easter Day, before the Matin service of which the crosses and pictures were uncovered. The veils are white, and marked with red crosses, to call our attention to the spotless but bloody Passion of our Lord. The commonest use in the Western Church is to begin this veiling at the first Vespers of Passion Sunday, and to employ violet veils without a cross or other device embroidered on them.

526. *Why is the sixth Sunday in Lent called Palm Sunday?*

In commemoration of the triumphal entry of our Lord into Jerusalem, when the people cut down branches of palm and strewed them in the way (*S. John* xii. 12).

527. *Are there any peculiar ceremonies in honour of this event?*

Yes; the churches are decked with palm, and there is a solemn procession before the chief celebration, in which palm-branches are carried. These are also held during the singing of the Holy Gospel.

528. According to old English use during the procession the rood (that is, the cross which surmounted the screen) was uncovered, and so remained exposed till Evensong, in token that in this triumphal procession Christ manifested forth His glory for a little while ere He drank still deeper of the cup of ignominy in His Passion. For a similar reason the churchyard cross was decked with flowers and evergreens, and the procession made a station there, and sang an appropriate anthem.

529. The hymn "Glory and laud and honour" is sung by seven boys, in allusion to the Hebrew children who cried Hosanna.

530. *Is it not customary to sing the Holy Week Gospels with peculiar ceremonies?*

It is; and you will observe that they are of great length, so as to form a very marked feature in the services. On Sunday S. Matthew's narrative of the Passion is recited; on Monday and Tuesday that of S. Mark; on Wednesday and Thursday that of S. Luke; and on Friday that of S. John. Whence the Holy Week Gospels were called the "Passions." The customary lights and incense are omitted; and it is usual, when there are sufficient clergy, for the Passion to be sung by three—one reciting the words of the Evangelist, another those of Christ, and a third those of the Jews and others; or at least for the deacon to sing these parts with different musical intonations. Another pious custom is for all to kneel down at the words which tell of the death of our Lord, while a short pause is made for private prayer. And the usual response, " Glory be to Thee, O Lord," etc., is omitted.

531. The Lenten veil, which hung between the choir and the altar, was suffered to fall at the words "the veil of the Temple was rent in the midst"; and on Good Friday at the words "They parted My raiment among them," two acolytes removed the two linen cloths which covered the slab of the altar.

532. *Why is the altar sometimes vested in white on Maundy Thursday?*

With reference to the Institution of the Blessed Sacrament. According to old English use, however, red,[1] the colour for times of more solemn penitence, was employed on this and the two following days. For the same reason the deacon and subdeacon resume their dalmatic and tunic. At Vespers, however, the altar is stripped, and remains so till the first service of Easter, and during this time the bells are not rung.

---

[1] These vestments of red for penitential times were very frequently trimmed with black to express at once the kingly nature of Him whose humiliation we commemorate, and our own sorrow for His sufferings—the royalty of His Passion and the wickedness which brought it about.

533. The three last days of Holy Week have ever been observed with extraordinary solemnity, as covering the hours actually occupied by the Passion of our Lord. Formerly the *Gloria Patri* was omitted at the Psalms, and the choir service began at once with the antiphon before the Psalms; and at the Nocturns, or night service, fifteen (or according to English use twenty-four) candles were arranged in a triangular candlestick at the Epistle side of the altar, which were extinguished one by one as the Psalms were recited in Matins and Lauds; the candles on the altar being also extinguished at the *Benedictus*. One candle was not extinguished, but was hidden behind the altar, while the fifty-first Psalm was recited in a low voice; after which it was restored to its place at the top of the candlestick. This service was called, from the extinguishing of the lights, the *Tenebrae*, or darkness, and symbolized the darkness which covered the whole earth at the time of our Lord's Crucifixion, and the desolation and abandonment which our Saviour endured in His Passion. The last candle was not extinguished, but was hidden awhile, and then reinstated, because God did not leave our Lord's soul in hell, nor suffer His Holy One to see corruption, but raised Him from the dead.

534. The altars were formerly *washed* with wine and water on Maundy Thursday, in memory of the act of S. Mary Magdalene, who washed our Lord's feet, and wiped them with the hair of her head, in preparation for His burial (*S. Matt.* xxvi. 12). And it was customary for bishops and superiors of religious houses to wash the feet of twelve or thirteen poor persons. The kings of England long performed this office, the last who did so being King James II. It was afterwards performed in the Chapel Royal by the Archbishop of York, acting for the sovereign; but since 1731 has been suffered to fall into disuse. Doles, however, are still distributed by the sovereign on this day.

535. *Why is there no celebration on Good Friday?*

The Church has from very early times been wont to stay on this day her memorial sacrifice out of veneration to that bloody oblation which was then consummated; as also because the Eucharist must always be more or less of a joyful service, and so seemed out of character on this day of desolation and grief.

536. Formerly the Sacrifice was pleaded to-day as on all other days, but the *Consecration* (as the festal element) was lacking; that is to say, the Sacrifice was offered with the Blessed Sacrament which had been consecrated the day before. This was called the *Mass of the Presanctified*, and was celebrated by the Easterns every day in Lent except Saturday and Sunday, and by the Armenians on Holy Saturday as well. In the absence of reservation, the best ritualists hold that the course most consonant to the mind of the Church is to say the Ante-Communion Office only on Good Friday.

537. *Will you explain to me why the altar in many churches remains stripped on Good Friday?*

The custom has reference to the stripping off of our Lord's garments at the pillar, and to His hanging naked on the Cross. Stripping was also a sign of humiliation; and so, just as the Church on festivals puts on her "beautiful garments" (*Isa.* lii. 1), and makes her clothing of "wrought gold" (*Ps.* xlv. 14), so on this day of sorrow and abasement she "lays her robe from" her like the King of Nineveh in the great fast (*Jonah* iii. 6). But if the altar cannot be conveniently laid bare, or is richly ornamented in colours, it is usual to cover it with a *black* frontal.

538. *What are the "Reproaches"?*

A selection of anthems, partly founded on words in the prophecy of Micah (vi. 3, etc.), intermingled with a very ancient form of the *Kyrie Eleison* used in the Greek Church. They set forth "the exceeding ingratitude of His chosen people to our Blessed Lord, and of those who, by their sins, crucify Him to themselves afresh." After the Reproaches the hymn "Sing, my tongue, the glorious battle," which commemorates the Life and Passion of our Lord, is sung.

539. The Introit must always be more or less of a festal feature. (See par. 412.) During Passiontide the Church, to impart somewhat of a mournful aspect, omits the *Gloria*; but on this day the whole "Psalm of Entrance" is hushed. For the same reason the "Reproaches" are sung *kneeling*.

540. The "Three Hours' Agony," which is a devotion frequently observed on Good Friday, is not a liturgical service, but arose from the need of an exercise, to enable the faithful to spend the actual hours during which the Lord of Glory hung on the Cross in devout meditation and prayer. Such "devotions" are common on the Continent, and are expressly provided for in Edward VI's Acts of Uniformity.

provided they do not let or hinder the course of public worship.[1]

Matins having been sung at 9 a.m., at which hour it is believed that the scourging at the pillar took place, and the altar service being concluded about noon, when He was nailed to the Cross, the clergyman who is to conduct the devotion kneels at the faldstool where the Litany is wont to be sung, and begins by the Invocation of the Holy Trinity. The prayers and hymns that follow are intermingled with short sermons, generally on the Seven Words spoken by our Lord from the Cross, and are so arranged as to keep the mind fixed without weariness on the agony and death of our Lord, and to conclude at 3 p.m., at which hour our Lord gave up the ghost.

541. *Are there any peculiar observances connected with Easter?*

It is the custom to place a wax taper of great height and size at the Gospel side of the altar. This is called the *Paschal taper*. It is lighted every day at High Celebration and Evensong till Low Sunday, and thence on Sundays and festivals till Ascension Day, when it is removed after the Gospel. It typifies the glory and majesty of our Lord's Resurrection, and the spiritual joy with which we should celebrate it. Easter has always been observed with a solemn Octave, both because it is the direct Christian counterpart

---

[1] " Provided also that it shall be lawful for all men, as well in churches, chapels, oratories, or other places, to use openly any psalms or passages, taken out of the Bible, at any due time, not letting or omitting the Service, or any part thereof, mentioned in the said book."— See Burn's *Ecclesiastical Law*, vol. iii. ch. iv. 9, p. 251.

of the Jewish Passover (*Exod.* xii. 15, 16), and on account of its dignity as the "queen of feasts." For this reason the first Sunday after Easter is called Low Sunday, as being "a little lower" only than the feast itself. And many ritualists hold that the special anthems in place of the *Venite* (and some say, but with less reason, the proper psalms),[1] should be sung every day throughout the octave. To impress upon us the unity of the feast, though it lasts throughout the week, the antiphon, "This is *the day* which the Lord has made: we will rejoice and be glad in it," is sung in place of the hymn up to the first Evensong of Low Sunday. Another observance is the frequent introduction of the triumphant "Alleluia" during the Easter season.

542. The Church requires all her children to communicate three times in the year, of which Easter, on account of its dignity and its relation to the Passover, is to be one.

543. The special observance of the Monday and Tuesday in Easter and Whitsun weeks would seem to have reference to the work of the Holy Trinity in the Resurrection and Descent of the Holy Ghost. Formerly Wednesday was so observed also (thus preserving the same truth, without counting in the feast-day itself); and perhaps for a similar reason, as well as to commemorate the three classes of martyrs—those in will and in deed, those in will though not in deed, and those in deed though not in will—the Church so early set apart the *three days* after Christmas as special festivals.

---

[1] See pars. 544-9 on the proper psalms for feasts.

CEREMONIES PECULIAR TO SEASONS 193

544. Does not the Church interrupt her monthly course of psalmody on certain feasts?

Yes, on the three great festivals, for the sake of greater dignity; and on Ascension Day, as the next in rank; on Ash Wednesday, in order to introduce the seven Penitential Psalms, "the seven weapons wherewith to oppose the seven deadly sins"; and on Good Friday, as the solemn memorial of the Death of Christ.

545. On *Christmas Day* the 19th Psalm is used with reference to the Birth of our Lord, the true Sun of Righteousness, Who then "came forth as a bridegroom," wedded to our humanity, "out of His chamber," the Virgin's womb, "rejoicing as a giant to run His course" of sorrow and humiliation, to save a ruined world; the 45th, as telling of that "girding with the sword," namely our flesh, with which He would conquer Satan, and crush his empire over the human race; the 85th, as speaking of "righteousness and peace kissing each other," that is, offended justice being satisfied, and our "peace" being made by the Incarnation and subsequent oblation of our Lord; the 89th, as foretelling the subduing of Egypt, that is, the empire of Satan, by the mighty arm of our Incarnate Lord; the 110th, as referring to "the dew of" our Lord's "birth"; and the 132nd, as telling of the habitation "for the mighty God of Jacob," viz. the substance of our flesh.

546. On *Good Friday* the 22nd Psalm foretells the Passion of Christ; the 40th speaks of the "innumerable troubles" that "came about" Him on the way of sorrows and the weight of our "sins"—which He made as it were His own—taking "such hold upon" Him that He was "not able to look up"; the 54th tells us of that mighty oblation, that "offering of a free heart"—the great sacrifice—which our Lord

o

made of Himself on Calvary; the 69th, which is sung in the evening, speaks of that "rebuke" of God which "broke" His "heart," when He cried in bitterness of soul, "My God, My God, why hast Thou forsaken Me?"; the 88th, of those "wonders among the dead," when He went and "preached to the spirits in prison" (1 *S. Pet.* iii. 19); and then looks forward to Easter morning: "Shall the dead rise up again, and praise Thee?"

547. The Matin Psalms at *Easter* speak of "the breaking of" the bonds of the rulers "asunder," when our Lord brake through the sealed stone, and passed by the astonished keepers; of the awakening "right early"—even when it was yet dark; of the showing His people the power of His works, when He appeared to S. Mary Magdalene and to the other disciples. The Evening Psalms recount the resurrection of Christ the humbled Man, the Sinless One, "out of the dust" of death; the driving back of Jordan, a type of the bursting of the gates of Death; the stone which the builders refused, viz. Him whom the rulers of the Jews rejected, becoming the Headstone in the corner.

548. On *Ascension Day* the Church tells in her psalmody of the "glory" of Christ being "set above the heavens"; and of His being crowned with glory and worship "at the right hand of God"; of His "dwelling" in the "tabernacle of God," even in the heaven of heavens, the "holy hill" of God; of God's setting "a crown of pure gold" upon His head; of the "King of Glory" entering, in triumphal majesty, through "the everlasting doors" of heaven; of His "going up" into heaven "with a merry noise," and there reigning "the King of all the earth"; and of His "setting up" Himself "above the heavens," and His "glory above all the earth," that His "beloved" —that is, His disciples—for whom He tasted death, "may be delivered."

549. On *Whitsun Day* the 48th Psalm tells of the Apostles waiting for the "loving-kindness" of God, even the promised gift of the Comforter, "in the midst of" Jerusalem, in the upper chamber, which had been the scene of the first Eucharist; the 68th, of the "gracious rain," the Spirit of God, which He sent upon His "inheritance," the Church; the 104th, of the "Breath" or Spirit of God, which He this day sent forth to "renew the face of the earth"; and the 145th, of that "declaring of the power" of God, when every one heard in his own tongue the wonderful works of God, and the "memorial of His abundant kindness" was showed by the adding to the Church of three thousand souls.

550. *What is Corpus Christi, or Eucharist Thursday?*

It is the first Thursday after Trinity Sunday, and was set apart in the Western Church in the thirteenth century in honour of the Mystery of our Lord's Presence in the Blessed Sacrament, because it was felt that this sacred Mystery could not be adequately commemorated on the day of its institution, which occurs in the midst of the mournful celebration of His Passion.

551. Corpus Christi, together with the feast of the Assumption of the Blessed Virgin, a festival which commemorates the falling asleep of the Blessed Virgin, and the commemoration of All Souls, though no longer of canonical obligation in our Church, may as lawfully be restored as free-will offerings of devotion, as such observances as Dedication Feasts or Harvest Festivals.
[B.]

552. *Why is the anniversary of the consecration of a church kept with so much solemnity?*

Because we should thank God for all the

benefits we and others derive from the services and the means of grace dispensed there; and as a type of the final triumph of the Church of Christ—the "great congregation" of those whom "no man can number"—to which the hymns and introit specially refer us.

553. All Saints' Day is similarly observed with solemnity, as a commemoration and anticipation of the final glory of all God's elect, when "the marriage of the Lamb" shall come, and "His Bride," the Church, having "made herself ready," shall be "arrayed in fine linen, clean and white, for the fine linen is the righteousness of saints (*Rev.* xix. 7, 8).

554. But since the triumph is not yet come, and because sin and weakness delay its approach, the Church was wont to observe the morrow of All Saints' Day as the commemoration of *all the Souls* of her children departed, praying that God would speedily accomplish the number of His elect, and would give to the souls of the departed rest and peace, "not remembering our offences, nor the offences of our forefathers." Whence there were two Evensongs on All Saints' Day, the second Vespers of All Saints being followed by the Vespers of the Dead. Churches are dedicated in honour of "All Souls" in token that they "are in the hand of God," and having "died in the Lord" are "blessed," even though they were not such bright and burning lamps in the Church of God as to have deserved to be enrolled in her catalogue of eminent saints. For the same reason it was the custom for the faithful to deck the graves of their friends and relations with flowers on this day. Though the public commemoration of All Souls' Day is not now insisted on by the Church of England, the day has

CEREMONIES PECULIAR TO SEASONS 197

ever been marked in the Kalendars, which till 1832 were a monopoly of the Stationers' Company, and received as such the sanction of the Archbishop of Canterbury;[1] and in every "Primer" or Manual of private devotion issued by authority, except the second of King Edward VI, issued in 1553, the *Dirge* or Service for the Departed (so called from the first word of the initial Antiphon in Latin—*Dirige*, " Direct Thou ") has found a place; a sufficient indication of the mind of the Church, that at Hallowtide we should remember *both* classes of the departed. (See pars. 317-9.)

555. All Saints' Day is the *last* of the Church's greater commemorations of her departed worthies, because it sums them all up in one, and because the final triumph of the saints and the marriage of the Lamb shall be at the *end* of time; just as Trinity Sunday is the last of her sacred seasons, because the Beatific Vision is the eternal *end* of the Church Triumphant, when time shall be no more.

---

[1] The other days were March 17, S. *Patrick ;* Thursday after Trinity Sunday, *Corpus Christi ;* July 7, *Translation of S. Thomas of Canterbury* ; August 15, *Assumption of the Blessed Virgin.* But the different editions of the Primer add others, and Queen Elizabeth's Latin Prayer Book has a saint for nearly every day in the year.

APPENDIX

SECTION XV

THE CANONICAL HOURS

556. *What are the Canonical Hours?*

They are services performed at certain hours of the day, by means of which the whole Psalter is recited every week. They were formerly said in parish as well as conventual churches, and by the "secular" as well as the "religious" clergy; but having come to be said in the former case by "accumulation," they were, on the reformation of the service-books, moulded into two services for public use, named after the two principal hours, *Matins* and *Evensong*, and the Psalter was so distributed to be said through monthly. At the same time services for the Hours were given for private recitation in the various editions of the "Primer." They are still observed in Sisterhoods and other Religious Houses.

557. *How many of these "Hours" are there?*

Seven; according to the saying of the psalmist, "Seven times a day do I praise Thee"

(*Ps.* cxix. 164). They are called Matins, Prime, Terce, Sext, Nones, Vespers, and Compline.[1]

558. *What is the service of Matins?*

A service formerly sung at midnight, according to the words of David, " At midnight I will rise to give thanks unto Thee " (*Ps.* cxix. 62); but now very frequently said late at night by anticipation, or at early morning. It consists of two distinct services, *Nocturns* (which belongs to the night-office) and Lauds, which is reckoned as the first of the " Day Hours."

559. On Sundays and festivals, according to the most usual arrangement, Matins consists of three Nocturns (comprising nineteen Psalms) and Lauds; on ordinary weekdays of one Nocturn of twelve Psalms and Lauds.

560. *Will you describe the service of Matins?*

The Lord's Prayer, the Angelic Salutation, and the Creed having been said privately, it commences with the ℣. *O Lord, open Thou my lips*, as in the public service. O God, make speed, etc., and the *Gloria* following : at the end of the *Gloria* is said " Alleluia," except from

---

[1] " We read that Sayntes, both in the Old Law and in the New, praysed God in these hours. Daniel the prophet worshipped God thrice in the day kneeling : that was, after the exposition of S. Jerome, at Terce, at Sext, and at None. Also Peter and John went up to the temple to pray at the hour of None, as it is written in the Acts of the Apostles. And S. Paul and Silas being in prison, prayed to God at midnight. . . ."—*Myrrours.*

Septuagesima to Easter, when *Praise be to Thee, O Lord, King of eternal glory*, is said instead. (See par. 518.) The other Hours (except Compline) begin in the same way, except that the Creed and the ℣. *O Lord, open Thou my lips*, are only said before Matins, as being the first service of the day.

561. *What is the Angelic Salutation?*

It is the passage of Holy Writ consisting of portions of the 28th and 42nd verses of the 1st chapter of S. Luke, and is so called because the first portion forms the salutation given by the angel to Mary at the Annunciation. It has long been used by Christians as a memorial of the Incarnation.[1]

562. *What follows after the Gloria and Alleluia?*

The Psalm *Venite* is sung intermingled with its anthem, which is called the Invitatory, and is sung by four, three, or two rulers, or by the precentor alone, according as the feast is distinguished as quadruple, triple, double, or simple invitatory.

---

[1] The *Angelus* is a form of prayer by way of memorial of the Incarnation, said three times a day at the sound of a bell, thence called the *Angelus-bell*. It consists of three antiphons, each followed by the Angelic Salutation, and the whole concluded by the collect for the feast of the Annunciation. According to old English use it was said *twice* daily, viz. when the bell rang for Prime (see par. 574), and when the curfew-bell rang at evening. At present, in most parts of the Continent, it is said at 6 a.m., noon, and 6 p.m.; but in some places (as in Italy) at sunrise, noon, and sunset.

THE CANONICAL HOURS

563. *How is the Invitatory sung?*

It is chanted entire before and after the Psalm and also after the 2nd, 7th, and last verses The second half is chanted after the 4th and 9th verses, and after the *Gloria*.

564. *What is the object of the Invitatory?*

Its object, like that of the whole Psalm, is to stir up or "invite" the people to join in the psalmody which is immediately to follow. The short sentence or anthem, which varies according to the season or festival, gives the keynote and makes the otherwise unvarying Psalm take the spirit of the particular occasion.

565. *Please to explain this more fully.*

I can best do so by giving a few instances. On Palm Sunday the Invitatory is "They have not known My ways, unto whom I sware in My wrath that they should not enter into My rest," thus pointing to the Jews not recognizing the Lord in His Passion, and so missing the rest that belongs to the true people of God; while on Easter Day it is "Alleluia, Alleluia, Christ hath risen to-day, Alleluia, Alleluia," thus showing that we are specially bidden to our psalmody to-day on account of our Lord's resurrection. So on the feast of an Apostle the Invitatory is "The Lord the King of the Apostles: O come let us worship"; on that of a martyr, "The righteous shall flourish, being planted in the house of the Lord: let us rejoice and be glad in His holy solemnity." On a virgin's day, "Come, let us worship Jesus Christ the Lamb: the spouse of virgin souls."

566. *Do the Psalms immediately follow?*

No, a hymn is first sung, and then the Psalms with their antiphons follow.

567. *Why does a hymn precede the Psalms?*

Mystical writers tell us that by hymns is to be understood the life of those who praise God in contemplation; by Psalms the conversation of those who praise Him in the deeds of active life; and that therefore in the Nocturn service, which is said in the night, a time more fit for contemplation than for work, the hymn comes before the Psalms to show that contemplative souls wait upon God while they that work are asleep, and prefer meditation before work; while at Lauds, which is said nearer the day, the Psalms are put before the hymn to show that they who would serve God must here work out their salvation and serve God by good deeds, that hereafter they may contemplate Him eternally in heaven.

568. *What are Antiphons?*

An antiphon is a verse, generally of Holy Scripture, which is sung before and after the Psalms and Canticles, and like the Invitatory gives the keynote to the Psalm. A few words only are sung before, while the whole antiphon is repeated after the Psalm in token that here we see only "in part," but hereafter "we shall see face to face."

569. *Will you give a few instances of Antiphons?*

On Passion Sunday the antiphon to the first Psalm is "Foxes have holes, and birds of the air have nests, but the Son of Man hath not where to lay His head"; while on Easter Day it is "I am that I am, and my counsel is not with the wicked; but my delight is in the law of the Lord, alleluia." On the feast of a confessor it is taken from the Psalm itself, thus, "Blessed is the man who meditates in the law of the Lord, whose will remaineth therein day and night, and whatsoever he doeth it shall prosper." By this means the same Psalm is made to apply to the Passion and Resurrection of our Lord, and to the blameless lives of those who have witnessed a good confession for Him.

570. *How are the Psalms arranged at Matins?*

The Psalter is commenced on Sunday, when Psalms 1–21 are sung, omitting 4 and 5, which occur elsewhere. On Monday Psalms 27–38 are sung; on Tuesday Psalms 39–52; on Wednesday Psalms 53–68, omitting 54, 63, 65, 67; on Thursday Psalms 69–81; on Friday Psalms 81–97, omitting 90, 93, and 95; and on Saturday Psalms 98–109.

571. *What occurs at Matins after the Psalms?*

At the end of each division or nocturn occurs a versicle with its response. The Lord's Prayer, etc., are then said silently, and the reader, having first asked a blessing from the officiant, reads a lesson, at the end of which a responsory is sung. In this way three lessons are said at each nocturn. At the end of the ninth lesson on Sundays and feasts out of Advent, Septuagesima, Lent, and the Ember weeks, the *Te Deum* follows; but at those times the ninth responsory is repeated in its place, and Lauds follow immediately.

572. *Will you describe the arrangement of Lauds?*

After a versicle and response proper to the season it begins with *O God, make speed*, etc., as at Matins. After the *Gloria* and Alleluia five portions of Psalms follow, each portion with its antiphon. Of these the first Psalm on Sundays is the 93rd, on Wednesdays the 51st; the second varies with each day; the third is always the 63rd and 67th, said under one *Gloria* and antiphon; the fourth, the Canticle, *O all ye works of the Lord*, on Sundays; and on weekdays another Canticle from the Old Testament; and the fifth, Psalms 148-50, said under one *Gloria* and antiphon. After the Psalms a verse is chanted for the chapter, to which the choir replies *Thanks be to God*. Then follows the hymn with its versicle and response; the *Bene-*

dictus with its proper antiphon, which on double feasts is said entire before as well as after its canticle. On festivals the collect immediately follows, prefaced by *The Lord be with you*, etc.; but on ferial days certain versicles and responses are first said kneeling.

573. *Why does the officiant go to the sanctuary step to say the collect?*

Because it is taken from the Communion Service, and is therefore the Eucharistic and sacrificial feature in the choir services. For the same reason when the service is said solemnly the taper-bearers with lighted tapers stand on either side.

574. *What is Prime?*

It is a service sung at 6 a.m. or thereabouts, the hour in which our Lord was led before Pilate and accused, and in which after His Resurrection He appeared to S. Mary Magdalene; and is called Prime from the Latin *Prima* (*scil. hora*), "the first hour," because the hours of the day were formerly reckoned from 6 a.m. For the same reason the 9 o'clock service is called *Terce*, or "the third hour"; that at midday *Sext*, or "the sixth hour"; and that at 3 p.m. *Nones*, or "the ninth hour."

575. *How is Prime arranged?*

According to the old English arrangement called "of Sarum," after the usual versicles and hymns, Psalms 22–26 are sung, followed by Psalm 54. On Sundays (except between Septuagesima and Easter, when Psalm 93 is substituted) follows Psalm 118. The first thirty-two verses of Psalm 119, sung in two portions of sixteen verses, concluding the psalmody both on Sundays and weekdays. These are all sung under one antiphon. The Creed of S. Athanasius follows with its own antiphon. Then follows a verse for the chapter as at Lauds, the responsory *Lord, have mercy*, Lord's Prayer, Creed, sundry versicles and responses, the Confession and Absolution, some further versicles, and the collect.

576. According to the Roman use, Psalm 54 is first said, followed on Sunday by Psalm 118 or 93, as above; the Psalms 22–26 are distributed among the other days of the week except Saturday; and the Athanasian Creed is only said on Sundays and without a separate antiphon.

577. There were several forms of the Hour services. The most celebrated is the Mosaic arrangement, instituted by S. Benedict in the sixth century, but derived by him from the Egyptian hermits. That best known and most widely used in England, however, was the use or arrangement called "of Salisbury," because it was made (or rather consolidated) by S. Osmund, bishop of that city.[1] In their main features the various Western uses agree—in the general form of the services, in the greater dignity of Lauds and Vespers, and in the frequent use of the 119th Psalm, which formed the staple

---

[1] The services are here described according to the "use of Salisbury," as this use is generally followed in the English Religious Houses.

of the lesser hours. The chief peculiarity of the monastic use (which is probably the *oldest* arrangement of the Psalter) consisted in the greater number of Psalms assigned to Nocturns, in the singing of Psalm iii at the beginning of the night-office before the *Venite*, and in the assignment of four *Psalms* only to Vespers instead of *five* as elsewhere; a trace of which remains in our present use of the 119th Psalm.[1]

578. *What is Terce?*

A service for 9 a.m., the hour in which the Holy Ghost is believed to have fallen upon the Apostles—an event commemorated in the hymn —and also that in which our Lord was scourged and crowned with thorns.

579. For the first of these reasons the hymn " Come, Holy Ghost, our souls inspire " is sung during the Whitsun octave in place of the usual

---

[1] The reason for this division would appear to be as follows :— Matins, being sung in the daytime, represents our life of probation here, during which we brace ourselves up to our labour by contemplating the Passion of our Lord, in which He received His *five* wounds. But Evensong, which is sung at nightfall, represents the "rest that remaineth for the people of God," when we shall join in that perpetual " service of song " before the throne of God in the New Jerusalem, the city that " lieth four-square " (*Rev.* xxi. 16); so too, in our active life here on earth, we attain to holiness by watching over and consecrating our *five* senses ; while in our life of contemplation in glory we shall rejoice before God in the *four* transcendent attributes of the resurrection body—clarity, agility, impassibility, and subtlety. The curious reader will remember that between the tabernacle and the court were *five* pillars of shittim wood overlaid with gold (*Exod.* xxvi. 37), but between the Holy and the Most Holy Place *four* (ibid. *v.* 32). Five Psalms would appear to have been later assigned to Vespers to make it correspond more closely with Lauds, of which it is the counterpart, as Compline is of Prime.

hymn for Terce, and is accompanied by special solemnities.[1]

580. *Will you describe the arrangement of Terce?*

It begins precisely as Prime, with *O God, make speed*, the *Gloria* and Alleluia; then the hymn; after that six portions of Psalm 119 (verses 33–80), each two portions under one *Gloria*; and the whole under one antiphon. A verse for the chapter, a responsory, and the collect, which, however, on weekdays is preceded by the ninefold *Lord, have mercy*, the Lord's Prayer, sundry versicles, and the 51st Psalm.

581. *What is Sext?*

The services for noon, the hour in which our Lord was nailed to the Cross. Its arrangement is precisely the same as that of Terce. It has its proper hymn and its own six portions of Psalm 119 (verses 81–128).

582. *What is Nones?*

The service for 3 p.m., the hour in which our Lord yielded up the ghost on the Cross; it follows the order of Terce and Sext, having its own hymn and the remaining six portions of Psalm 119 (verses 129 to end).

---

[1] "In die Pentecostes incipiat executor officii horam tertiam ad gradum chori, et tunc procedat cum ceteris sacerdotibus thuribulis precedentibus ad gradum altaris, et ibi omnes simul incipiant hymnum 'Veni Creator Spiritus' genuflectendo . . . tunc surgentes thurificent altare."—*Crede Michi*, fol. xiii.

583. In the Benedictine order four portions of the 119th Psalm (verses 1–32) are said on Sundays at Prime; and three portions at each of the other lesser hours on Sunday and Monday; on weekdays at Prime three Psalms are said in order, beginning with Psalms 1, 2, and 6, on Monday, and carrying on the Psalter to Psalm 21, with which the Sunday Matins is commenced. On Tuesday and the remaining weekdays Psalms 120–22 are said at Terce; 123–25 at Sext; and 126–28 at Nones.

584. *What is Vespers?*

Vespers, called also Evensong, is a service for 6 p.m., the hour in which our Lord was taken down from the Cross, and in which also on Maundy Thursday He celebrated the Last Supper and instituted the Holy Eucharist.

585. *How is this service arranged?*

It resembles Lauds in its general arrangement. Immediately after the *Gloria* and Alleluia there follow five Psalms, each with its *Gloria*. These are said sometimes under one antiphon (as on the weekdays in Eastertide and at the first Vespers of most feasts), sometimes each with its own antiphon. The chapter (followed at certain times by the responsory), the hymn with its versicle and response, and the *Magnificat* with its proper antiphon (which like that to the *Benedictus* is "doubled" [see par. 572] on the second Vespers of all "double" feasts, and at *both* Vespers of principal doubles) follow; and lastly is said the collect, which in the ferial service is preceded by certain versicles and responses as at the other hours.

586. In the Roman rite the antiphons (both to Psalms and Canticles) are "doubled" at Matins, Lauds, and both Vespers of double feasts.

587. *How are the Psalms arranged at Vespers?*

The Sunday services take the Psalter up where the Saturday Matins left it, at Psalm 110, and carries it to Psalm 115. Psalms 116–21 are said on Monday (omitting 118, which occurs in the Sunday Prime, and 119, which is said in the lesser day hours); on Tuesday, Psalms 122–26; on Wednesday, 127–31; on Thursday, 132–37 (omitting 134, which occurs at Compline); on Friday, 138–42; and on Saturday, 144–47 (the latter in two divisions). Psalms 148–50, which complete the Psalter, are sung at Lauds.

588. In the Benedictine order four Psalms or portions of Psalms are sung at Vespers in the following order: Sunday, 110–13; Monday, 114, 115, under one *Gloria*, 116, 117, 129; Tuesday, 130–33; Wednesday, 135–38; Thursday, 139, in two divisions, 140, 141; Friday, 142, 143, 144, in two divisions; Saturday, 145, in two divisions, 146, 147, to verse 12, under one *Gloria*, 147, verse 12.

THE CANONICAL HOURS

589. *What are Memorials?*

They consist of an antiphon, versicle, response, and collect, said in commemoration of a certain mystery or of a particular saint, and occur after the collect for the day at Lauds and Vespers.

590. If two feasts "occur" the lesser is commemorated by (1) the antiphon proper to *Benedictus* (or at Vespers to *Magnificat*) on such feast; (2) the versicle and response attached to its proper hymn; and (3) its collect. Besides these, there are ordinary memorials, such as of S. Mary, All Saints, the Cross, etc.

591. *What is Compline?*

The service which *completes* the daily course of hours; hence the name (*completorium*, *complendum*, that which fulfils or closes). It belongs to 9 p.m., the hour in which our Lord was buried, and in which also He suffered His agony in the garden.

592. *How is Compline arranged?*

The officiant before beginning *O God, make speed* in a loud voice, says, in a somewhat lower tone, *Turn us, O God our Saviour*, to which the rest reply, *And let Thine anger cease from us*. This is done to ask pardon for whatsoever has been done amiss throughout the day. The service then proceeds as at Vespers. The Psalms (4th, 31st to verse 6, 91st, 134th) are said under one antiphon, and the last two Psalms under one *Gloria*. The hymn with its versicle and response, and the *Nunc Dimittis* with its antiphon follow. And the service is concluded with the ninefold *Lord, have mercy*, the Lord's Prayer, Creed, sundry versicles (and in the weekday service the 51st Psalm), and the collect *Lighten our darkness*.

593. The Roman order of Compline differs somewhat in arrangement. The service commences by the reader begging the benediction of the superior, which given, the short lesson (1 *S. Peter* v. 8) follows; then *Our help is in the Name of the Lord*, etc., the Lord's Prayer, the Confession and Absolution. Then *Turn Thou us, O God our Saviour*, as in the Sarum office. The four Psalms as above, each with its *Gloria*. According to this order, the antiphon never varies (except in Eastertide, when a thrice-repeated Alleluia is substituted). The hymn is also invariable; and the versicles before the collect are not said on double feasts or within octaves. The collect is different, and there are one or two minor variations. In the Benedictine use there are only three Psalms, and *Nunc Dimittis* is not said.

594. *What are the petitions "for the peace of the Church"?*

They consist of Psalm 123, followed by *Lord, have mercy*, the Lord's Prayer, some versicles, and a collect, said daily (except on double feasts and in certain octaves, and from Christmas Eve to the second Sunday after Epiphany,

THE CANONICAL HOURS

and from Maundy Thursday to the first Sunday after Trinity) after Lauds and Compline.

595. During the same time, Psalm 121, "I will lift up mine eyes," is said after Prime. Neither of these Psalms are so used in the Roman or Benedictine orders, but according to the latter at the end of Prime Psalm 130, "Out of the deep," is said for the faithful departed.

596. *Do the services vary at different seasons?*

There are proper antiphons, chapters, responsories, and collects for the seasons, and for the feasts of saints, and at Matins, Lauds, and Vespers proper hymns. But the structure of the service is the same except on the three last days of Holy Week, and in the Easter octave.

597. *How do the services differ on the three last days of Holy Week?*

After the Lord's Prayer, etc., have been said in silence, they begin directly with the antiphon to the Psalms; the Psalms follow without any *Gloria*; all chapters and hymns are omitted; and the service concludes with *Lord, have mercy*, the 51st Psalm, and the collect "Almighty God, we beseech Thee to behold this Thy family."

598. *What is the object of these variations?*

To mark better our sense of sorrow and desolation at the Passion of our Lord.

599. *How are the services arranged in the Easter octave?*

The versicles, *O God, make speed*, etc., are resumed; but there is no hymn, chapter, or responsory at any of the hours. In place thereof this versicle and response are said at Lauds: "The Lord is risen from the tomb. ℟. Who died to save us from our doom, Alleluia"; and at the other hours this antiphon, "This is the day which the Lord hath made; we will rejoice and be glad in it." To this sundry versicles and responses are added at Vespers. The antiphons, versicles, responsories, etc., are said with "Alleluia" from now to Trinity Sunday.

"Ye shall reverence My sanctuary."

INDEX

The figures refer to paragraphs, not to pages. Ceremonies alluded to in the work which are now obsolete are marked with an asterisk.

A

Ablutions, 397–404.
Absolution, 325–27.
   ,,   (Sacramental), why ministered in violet stole, 485.
Abstinence and fasting, distinction between, 148, 149.
   ,,   why Friday set apart as a day of, 150.
Access, prayer of humble, 340.
   ,,   why communicants only mentioned in, 341.
* "Accumulation," 208.
Acolytes, why boys serve as, 281.
Acolytes' candlesticks, 49.
Address, prayer of. (See "Prayer of Humble Access.")
Adoration (Eucharistical), 359.
   ,,   Bp. Ridley on, 359.
   ,,   ,, Forbes on, 359.
   ,,   ,, Jeremy Taylor on, 359.
   ,,   not forbidden by Article xxviii, 360.
Advent, 138–40.
   ,, colour of vestments in, 101–04.
   ,, meaning of, 139.
   ,, why dalmatic and tunic not used in, 95, 506.
   ,, why marriages forbidden during, 484.
   ,, why *Te Deum* not used in, 229.
   ,, why year begins with, 502.
Agnus Dei, what, and why sung, 444.
   ,, how varied in mortuary celebrations, 465.
Agony (Devotion of the Three Hours), on Good Friday, 540.
Alb (choral), 66.
   ,,   ,, when and why worn, 67, 68.

Alb (Eucharistic), 81.
,, ,, of what symbolical, 82.
,, ,, why celebrant preaches in his, 430.
*Alleluia, "farewell to," 518.
,, why not sung in Lent, 518.
,, why sung in Hebrew, 518 (note).
All Saints' Day, 553.
,, why last of the Church's yearly commemorations, 555.
All Souls' Day, 554.
,, why churches dedicated to, 554.
,, why graves decked on, 554.
"All the whole Church," 383.
Alms, why removed from the Altar, 302.
,, why mentioned with the oblations in the Prayer for Church Militant, 303.
Altar, 14-18.
,, bowing at the, 198.
,, why called the Lord's Table, 346.
,, why furnished with cross and candles, 21, 22.
,, why made so conspicuous, 16, 17.
,, why made of wood or stone indifferently, 347.
,, why placed at east end, 14.
,, why railed off, 15.
Ambrosian tones, 211.
Amen, why sung in Hebrew, 518 (note).
Amice, 79.
,, its symbolic meaning, 80.
Andrewes (Bishop) on the Eucharistic Sacrifice, 284.
Angelic Salutation, the, 561.
Angelus, what, and when said, 561 (note).
Anointing of the sick, 486.
Antependium, or Altar frontal, 18.
Anthem, 250.
,, why the office hymn should serve as the, 250.
Antiphonal chanting, 192.
Antiphons, 568.
Apostles, feasts of, 154.
Arrangement and ornaments of the Church. [Sect. ii, p. 6.]
Article xxxi does not condemn the word "Mass," nor the primitive doctrine thereof, 284.
Ascension Day, 138-40.
,, ,, colour of vestments on, 101-04.
,, ,, proper Psalms for, why chosen, 548.

INDEX 217

Ascensiontide, why marriages not celebrated during, 484.
Ash Wednesday, 521.
,, ,, proper Psalms for, why chosen, 522.
Aspersion of blessed or "holy" water, what signified by, 115, 126.
Augustine (S.), on funeral celebrations, 452.
Aurora (or daybreak) Mass at Christmas, 409.

B

Banners, why employed in processions, 267.
,, of the Lion and of the Dragon, how and why used in old English rite, 268.
Banns of marriage, why announced in Solemn Celebrations, 430.
Baptism, conditional, 473.
,, why it cannot be repeated, 473.
,, why "solemnly" administered on Easter and Whitsun Eves, 472.
,, why two stoles (violet and white) used in administering, 467.
Baptismal shell, 54.
Bason and napkin for the lavabo, 41.
Benedict (S.) appointed five Psalms at Lauds and four at Evensong, 577.
,, derived his division of the Psalter from the Egyptian hermits, 577.
,, ordered the Lord's Prayer to be said aloud at Matins and Vespers, 242.
Benediction, why the ornaments of the Church and ministers are set apart by a form of, 110, 111.
Benedictions. [Section iv, p. 33.]
Benedictus, why incense is used at, 234-39.
,, ,, ,, less frequently than at *Magnificat*, 235 (note).
,, *qui venit*, what, and why sung, 440.
"Betrothal" in marriage, 476.
,, why performed in body of the church, 476.
Bezaleel, 8.
Biretta, 107.
Bishops Andrewes, Cosin, and Overall on Eucharistic Sacrifice, 284.
,, at Savoy Conference on Sign of the Cross, 243.
,, ,, on turning of the Priest from the people, 301.

218 THE RITUAL REASON WHY

Black, why used at funeral celebrations, 457.
,, one of the ecclesiastical colours, 101.
*Blessed bread, 118, 119.
Blue, how and why employed in old English rite, 104, 105.
,, cassocks, 59.
"Board (God's)," 347.
Bonnet of Jewish High Priest, 108.
Book of the Gospels, why censed, 429.
"Bounden duty and service (this our)," 387.
Bowing at the Altar, 198.
Boy, why server is generally a, 281.
*"Boy Bishop," 513.
Bread (breaking of the) in Canon, 354.
,, ,, the second time after the Consecration, 372.
,, in the Eucharist, why it must be the purest wheat bread, 307.
Brevint, the Mass a "Sacramental Passion," 393 (note).
Brown, how and why employed in old English rite, 104, 105.
Bucer on manual gestures, 339.
,, wished to make Sunday and festival reception compulsory, 343.
Burial of the Dead, why celebrated with "clerks," 491.
,, why cross used in the, 495.
,, why incense, 494.
,, why tapers, 496.
Burse, the, 37.

C

Cadence (in Gregorian tones), 213.
Candlemas Day, why so called, 515.
Candles, why distributed on the Purification, 515.
,, why placed on the Altar, 22.
Candlestick, the Paschal, 47.
Candlesticks, acolytes', 49.
Canonical Hours, the. [Section xv, p. 198.]
"Canon," what, and why so called, 344.
Cantoris side of the choir, 193.
,, why it leads, 200.
Carols, why sung at Christmas, 512.
Cassock, Bishop's, why violet, 59.
,, Chorister's, colour of, 59.
,, what, and what it signifies, 57, 58.
Celebrates once a day (why a Priest only), 409.

INDEX

Celebration, High. [See Section xi, p. 145.]
,, what it is, 410.
,, why incense is used at, 415.
,, Low, 274 [and Section x throughout, p. 86.]
,, loud responses out of character with, 324 (note 2).
Censer, 48.
Censing of choir, 237.
Ceremonies peculiar to certain seasons. [Section xiv, p. 175.]
Chalice, 33.
,, (mixed), its meaning, 304-06.
,, veil, what, and why used, 34.
,, formerly used by the acolyte to hold the paten in during certain parts of the service, 35.
Chancel, why severed off from rest of church, 12.
,, screen, why surmounted by a cross, 13.
Chanting from side to side, 192.
Chasuble, 88.
,, its meaning, 89.
,, why laid aside in preaching, 430.
,, why placed on the Altar, 430.
,, why it has a cross behind and a pillar in front, 90.
Choir, censing of, 237.
,, why faces eastward at *Glorias*, 196.
,, why sings from side to side, 192.
,, why vested in white, 55.
,, rulers of the, 202-06.
,, ,, why they sit at the Psalms, 205.
,, ,, why they vary in number, 204.
,, ,, why they wear copes, 205.
Choral tippet, 73.
Chrism, 131.
Christmas, 138-40.
,, colour of vestments, 101, 104.
,, decorations, 514.
,, midnight Mass at, 409, 511.
,, proper Psalms, why chosen, 545.
,, Day, why three High Celebrations are sung on, 409, 511.
Christmastide, why carols sung at, 512.
,, why marriages forbidden in, 484.
Chrysostom (S.), on communicating fasting, 405.
,, on Christian names, 469.
,, on funeral celebrations, 452.

Chrysostom (S.), on neglect of Communion, 360.
Church, arrangement and ornaments of the. [Section ii, p. 6.]
,, was wont to require all to assist at the Eucharist on Sundays and festivals, 342.
Churches, why consecrated, 128.
Churching of women, 500, 501.
Ciborium, what and how used, 31, 32.
Cincture, 58.
Classes of feasts, 156, 158–72.
,, of Sundays, 173, 174.
Claydon, sanctus-bell at, 336 (note).
Clement, Cyril, etc. (SS.), mention the *Lavabo*, 314.
Clergy buried in their vestments, why, 499.
,, why bound to say Matins and Evensong daily, 188, 189.
Clergyman, why the same cannot celebrate twice a day, 409.
"Cloke" (S. Paul's), 7 (note).
"Cloth (fair linen)," 381.
Collect, why the Priest should stand at, 248.
,, why said at Epistle corner, 292.
Colour of vestments explained, 100–05.
Colours, the ecclesiastical, 19, 20.
,, how and why employed, 101.
,, the old English or Sarum, 102.
,, ,, how and why employed, 104, 105.
Commemoration of the dead, 318, 385.
,, ,, why made with disjoined hands, 317.
,, of the living, 317.
Commemorations, why made in silence, 320.
"Common of Saints," 252.
Communicate fasting, why we should, 405.
,, once a day, why one can only, 409.
Communion cloth, 53, 378.
,, fasting, antiquity of, 405, 406.
,, ,, believed to have been ordered by S. Paul, 407.
,, ,, Bishop Jeremy Taylor on, 405.
,, ,, S. Chrysostom on, 405.
,, in one kind, 363, 364.
,, of the people, 375–79.
,, spiritual, 380.
Compline, one of the "hours of prayer," 591–94.
Compton (Long), sanctus-bell at, 336 (note).

INDEX

"Conditional" Baptism, 473.
Confession, why sometimes said by the Communicants only, 323.
Confessions, why Priest uses a violet stole in hearing, 485.
Consecration, 351.
,, actions connected with explained, 352–58.
,, of a Church (anniversary of), why observed, 552.
,, of Bishops, 135.
,, of Churches, Cemeteries, etc., 128–33.
,, why the Priest kneels after each, 358, 362.
Cope, what, 69.
,, when used, 70.
,, of what symbolical, 71.
,, why worn by rulers of the Choir, 205.
Corporal, what, and why used, 36, 286.
Corporas case, 37.
Corpse, censing of the, in funeral celebrations, 462.
Corpus Christi, 550.
Cosin (Bishop), on Eucharistic Sacrifice, 284.
Cotta, a variety of the surplice, 62, 279.
Council of Trent (Catechism of the) at one with Article xxviii, 360 (note).
Cowl, 109 (note).
Cranmer wished to translate the Office hymns, 250.
Credence, 25.
,, why the elements are prepared at the, 26.
Creed, why last two clauses inflected, 241.
,, why sign of the Cross made at end of, 243.
,, (Nicene), why reverences are made at "and was made man," 299.
,, ,, at "worshipped and glorified," 299.
,, ,, why sign of the Cross made at end of, 243.
Crib (Christmas), or "bambino," 513.
Cross, processional, 50.
,, ,, why in old English use one of wood painted red prescribed for Lent, and one of crystal for Eastertide, 266.
,, sign of, 243 (and note), 244.
,, why worked on chasuble, 90, 91.
,, why placed on the Altar, 21.
,, why used at funerals, 495.
,, why used in processions, 265.
Crosses, why five are marked on the fair linen cloth, 23.
Cyril, Clement, etc. (SS.), mention the *Lavabo*, 314.
,, (S.), on posture of Communicants, 378.

D

Dalmatic, 92.
,,   why laid aside in preaching, 430.
,,   why not laid on the Altar, 430.
,,   why not worn in penitential seasons, 95, 506.
,,   why resumed on Maundy Thursday, 509.
,,   why resumed on Mid-Lent Sunday, 508.
,,   why resumed on third and fourth Sundays in Advent, 508.

Damascene (S. John), on posture of Communicants, 378.
Daniel the Prophet prayed at the "hours of prayer," 557 (note).
Daybreak, Christmas Mass at, 409.
"Days of Obligation," 388, 389.
Deacon, dress of, 92, 94.
,,   why a Priest frequently acts as, 474 (note).
,,   why he ascends at the Consecration, 443.
,,   why he ascends at the Creed, *Sanctus*, and *Gloria*, 421.
,,   why he lays aside his dalmatic in preaching, 430.
,,   why he ministers at the right of the Priest, 415.
,,   why he stands below the Celebrant, 421.

Dead (Commemoration of), why made with disjoined hands, 317.
,,   why prayed for *after* the Consecration, 317.

Decani side of choir, 193.
Decorations, Christmas, 514.
Dedication of the Church, feasts of the, 184.
Details (minute) in ritual, 338.
"Devotions," as distinct from Divine Service, recognized by Act of Uniformity, 540 (note).
,,   of the Three Hours' Agony, 540.

Dies Irae, 466.
*Diptychs, 319.
*Dirge, why so called, 554.
,,   contained in all the Primers except that of 1553, 554.

Dominant, or reciting note in Gregorian tones, 209.
,,   ,,   not to be confounded with the dominant in modern music, 209 (note).

Dominus vobiscum, or "The Lord be with you," 245.
,,   why Priest extends his hands at the, 246.

Doxology or *Gloria*, 195.
,,   bowing at the, 196.

INDEX

*Doxology or *Gloria*, formerly omitted on the three last days of Holy Week, 533.
,, why Choir face Eastward at, 196.
,, why sung full, 201.
" Duty and service (this our bounden)," 387.

E

Easter, 138-40.
,, anthems, 541.
,, colour of vestments at, 101, 104.
,, Eve, why Baptism "solemnly" administered on, 472.
,, Monday and Tuesday, why observed, 543.
,, proper Psalms at, why chosen, 547.
,, taper, why used, 541.
,, why all are required to communicate at, 542.
,, why marriages are restrained through the Octave, 484.
,, why the antiphon "This is the day" is sung, 541.
Ecclesiastical History a witness to symbolic worship, 8.
Edward VI's First Prayer Book on the sign of the Cross, 243 (note).
Eighty-fourth Psalm applied by Spiritual writers to the Blessed Sacrament, 375.
Elevation of Blessed Sacrament, 365-68.
,, mystical meaning of the twofold, 365.
Ember weeks, 141.
,, colour of vestments in, 101, 104.
,, why *Te Deum* is not used in, 229.
Ember week (Whitsun), why *Te Deum* used, 231.
Ending, in Gregorian tones, 213.
Epinikion, what, and why so called, 333.
Epiphany, 138-40.
,, colour of vestments in, 101, 104.
Epistle, why sometimes taken from the Old Testament, 297.
,, why sung by Subdeacon, 422.
,, (or south) side of the Altar, why Collect read at, 292.
,, ,, why Epistle read at, 294.
Eucharist, why so called, 282.
,, why special vestments are assigned to the, 77.
Eucharistic vestments, 76-94.
,, why worn, 77.
,, their origin, 78.
Eulogia, 118-20.
Evensong (Matins and). [Section vi, p. 53.]

Evensong (Matins and), object of, 187.
,, the more direct part begins with the Lord's Prayer, 194 (note).
,, why "daily," 188.
,, why so called, 186.
,, why sung, 191.
,, why the Priest to say "either privately or openly," 189.
,, why feasts have first and second, 165–67.

F

"Fair linen cloth" of the Altar, its meaning, 23.
,, why marked with five crosses, 23.
* "Farewell to Alleluia," the, 518.
Fasting and abstinence, distinction between, 148, 149.
Fasts, 143.
,, why vigils of feasts observed as, 146.
Feasts and Fasts. [Section v, p. 41.]
,, (double), what, and why so called, 159
,, ,, why they have two Evensongs, 165–67.
,, how they clash, 169–74.
,, of Martyrs, why red is used on, 101.
,, of "Obligation," 388, 389.
,, of our Lord, 152.
,, of the Apostles, 154.
,, of the Blessed Virgin, 153.
Feria, what, 178.
,, greater, 180–82.
Final, in Gregorian music, 209.
Fire, why blessed at Easter and Pentecost, 125.
Flowers, why set on the Altar, 22.
Font, why placed near the west door, 11.
Forbes (Bishop), on Eucharistical adoration, 359.
Fraction, or breaking of the Bread, 354, 372.
Friday, why set apart as a day of abstinence, 150.
,, (Good), Devotion of the Three Hours' Agony on, 540.
,, ,, proper Psalms for, why chosen, 546.
,, ,, why altar stripped on, 537.
,, ,, why no celebration on, 535.
,, ,, why Reproaches are sung by way of Introit, 538.
Frontal (of the Altar), 18.
Funeral celebrations, why black vestments worn in, 457.

INDEX

Funeral celebrations, why incense is not used at the Introit and Gospel, 461.
,, of infants, why white is used at, 498.
,, ,, why the cross is borne without the staff, 498.
,, palls, why marked with the cross, 495.
,, ,, why black is discouraged for, 497.
,, tapers, 496.
,, and mortuary celebrations. [Section xii, p. 159.]
Funerals, why incense is used in, 494.
,, why the Holy Eucharist is celebrated at, 451.

G

Genuflexion, why made after each consecration, 358, 362.
,, why made on passing before the Consecrated Sacrament, 198.
Gestures (manual) or position of hands. (See Hands.)
Girdle, 83.
,, its meaning, 87.
,, (monastic), 109 (note).
Gloria Patri, 195.
,, ,, bowing at the, 196.
,, ,, formerly omitted on the last three days of Holy Week, 533.
,, ,, why choir face East at, 196.
,, ,, why sung full, 201.
* ,, *in Excelsis* formerly omitted in penitential seasons, 99.
,, ,, why said after Post-Communion, 390.
"*God's Board*," 347.
Gospel, incense and lights at the, 239, 428.
,, ,, S. Jerome on, 239.
,, (or north) side of the Altar, why service begun at, 287.
,, why not finished with "Here endeth the Gospel," 296.
,, why sign of the Cross is made at the end of, 243.
,, why sung by the deacon, 422.
,, why sung facing north, 224 (note).
Gospels (Book of the) why incensed, 429.
Gradual, the, 425.
*Graves, why they were wont to be garnished on All Souls' Day, 554.
Green, one of the ecclesiastical colours, 101.
,, why used on ordinary Sundays, 101.
Gregorian modes, what, 209.

Q

Gregorian tones (the eight), 209, 210.
Grey, how and why employed in the old English rite, 104, 105.

H

Habit, monastic, 109 (note).
Habits, clergy and sisters buried in their proper, 499.
Hands (position of), or manual gestures:—
,, why disjoined at Commemoration of the Departed, 317.
,, why extended at "The Lord be with you," 246.
,, why extended at Collect, 293.
,, why first extended and then joined at *Nicene Creed*, 298.
,, why joined at "Let us pray," 247.
,, (position of) at Prayer for Church Militant explained, 316.
,, ,, at Preface, 337.
Hermits (the Egyptian) were wont to sing five Psalms at Lauds and four at Vespers, 577.
High Celebration, what, 410.
,, why incense used at, 415.
,, why three sung on Christmas Day, 409, 511.
"Holy Father," why these words omitted from Preface of Trinity Sunday, 332.
Holy, Holy, Holy. (See *Sanctus*.)
"Holy is His Name," why reverence is done at, 197.
"Holy loaf," 120.
Holy water, 112–17.
Holy Week Gospels, 530.
Hood, academical, 74.
,, monastic, 109 (note).
Hosanna, why sung in Hebrew, 518 (note).
"Hours of prayer," what, and why observed, 208, 556.
,, monastic arrangement of, 577.
,, our Matins and Evensong compiled from, 208.
,, Sarum arrangement of, 577.
,, Services for the, 556.
,, provided in the various editions of the Primer, 208.
,, still used in Religious Houses, 208.
Houselling cloth, 53, 378.
Hymn (the) at Matins and Evensong, 250–54. (See Office hymn.)

INDEX

I

Incense, lights, and vestments always used in Christian worship, 8.
,, why offered at the Oblation, 433.
,, why used at funerals, 494.
,, why used at High Celebrations, 415.
,, why used at the *Benedictus*, 234.
,, why used at the Consecration, 442.
,, why used at the Gospel, 428.
,, why used at the *Magnificat*, 234.
,, why not used at *Nunc Dimittis*, 239 (note).
,, why not used at the Introit and Gospel in funeral celebrations, 461.

"Intentions," what, 320 (note).
Intonation, 214.
,, how used and why, 215, 216.
Introit, what, and why sung, 412, 413.
Invitatory Psalm, or *Venite*, 199, 563.
Invocation (part of Canon), 350.
,, why the Oblations are uncovered at the end of the, 352.
* "Ite, Missa est," 392.

J

James and John (SS.), wore the Jewish mitre, 108.
Jerome (S.), on lights at the Gospel, 239.
Jews use lights at their reading of the Law, 239.

K

Kind, Communion in one, 363.
* Kneeling anciently omitted in the Paschal season, 420.
Kneels after each Consecration (why the Priest), 358, 362.
Kyrie (notation to), why varied at the fourth and seventh responses, 418.

L

Lauds, one of the "hours of prayer," 572, 573.
Lavabo, what, and why so called, 41, 314.
Leavened bread, why used by Eastern Church, 308.
Lectern, 43.
Lent, 138-40.
,, colour of vestments in, 101, 104.
,, meaning of, 139.
,, why "Alleluia" omitted during, 518.

Lent, why dalmatic and tunic not used in, 95, 506.
,, why *Te Deum* not used in, 229.
,, why marriages restrained during, 484.
,, (fourth Sunday in), why called *Refreshment Sunday*, 508.
,, ,, why dalmatic resumed on, 508.
Lenten-hearse, 46.
Lessons, the, 223-25.
,, why read from a lectern, 223.
,, why people sit during the, 226.
Let us give thanks unto our Lord God, meaning of, 329.
,, why the Priest joins his hands at, 329.
Lift up your hearts, meaning of, 329.
,, why Priest extends his hands at, 329.
* Lighted taper, why held by candidate for Baptism, 471.
Lights, 22.
,, standard, 44.
,, vestments, and incense always used in Christian worship, 8.
,, why used at *Benedictus*, 239.
,, why used at the Gospel, 239, 428.
,, why used at the *Magnificat*, 239.
,, why used at *Sanctus* and Canon, 439, 441.
,, why used in funerals, 496.
Linen (Altar), why marked by five crosses, 23.
Lips, why signed at the versicle, *O Lord, open Thou*, 194.
Litany. [Section viii, p. 79.]
,, in procession, 261.
,, ,, first religious service in Saxon England, 270.
,, when "solemnly" sung and why, 261, 262.
,, why recited outside the screen, 260.
"Liturgical" colours, 19, 20, 100-05.
Liturgy, why so called, 283.
,, of S. James quoted by S. Paul, 6 (note).
Location, Christ's Presence in the Sacrament not by way of, 360 (and note).
Long Compton, Warwickshire, sanctus-bell at, 336 (note).
Lord's Prayer, why sign of the Cross made at the end, 243.
,, ,, two last clauses sung with inflections, 241.
,, ,, after Communion, why chanted, 448.
,, Table, why the Altar is so called, 346.
,, ,, answers to the Table of Showbread, 347.
Loud responses out of character with Low Celebration, 324 (note 2).

INDEX

Low Celebration, what, 274.
        [See Section x, p. 86, throughout.]
,, Sunday, why so called, 541.

M

Magnificat, why incense is used at the, 234, 239.
Maniple, 85.
,, its meaning, 87.
Manual gestures, or position of hands, in ritual explained. (See Hands.)
Marriage, 475-84.
,, banns of, why announced in Solemn Celebration, 430.
,, (ring used in), its meaning, 480.
,, ,, why placed on fourth finger, 480.
,, ,, ,, left hand, 480.
,, why not solemnized in Advent, etc., 484.
,, why white vestments are used in solemnizing, 475.
Martyrs, why red is used on feasts of, 101.
Mary (Blessed Virgin), Feasts of the, 153.
,, why white is used on, 101.
Mass, meaning of the word, 282.
,, (midnight) at Christmas, 409, 511.
,, neither term nor true doctrine of condemned in Article xxxi, 284.
,, term applied to Communion Service in Edward's First Prayer Book, 285.
,, of the Presanctified, 536.
Matins and Evensong. [Section vi, p. 53.]
,, object of, 187.
,, the more direct part begins with the Lord's Prayer, 194 (note).
,, why "daily," 188.
,, why so called, 186.
,, why sung, 191.
,, why the Priest to say "either privately or openly," 189.
,, one of the "hours of prayer," 560-71.
Maundy Thursday, 532-34.
Mediation in Gregorian tones, 213.
Memorials, what, 255, 589.
Mental and vocal prayer, 320.
Midst of the altar, why Creed is said in the, 298.
Ministers, why they ascend at the Creed and *Gloria in Excelsis*, 421.

Ministers, why they stand at a High Celebration, 419.
,,   ,,   on different steps, 421.
,,   ornaments of the. [Section iii, p. 18.]
,,   why set apart by a form of benediction, 110, 111.
Minute details in ritual, 338.
Missah (or Sacrifice in the Eucharist), not condemned by Article xxxi, 284.
,,   ,,   ,,   taught by best English divines, 284.
Mitre, its meaning, 108.
,,   why cloven, 108.
,,   of Jewish High Priest, 108.
,,   ,,   ,,   worn by SS. James and John, 108.
Mixed chalice, its meaning, 304–06.
Modes (Gregorian), the fourteen, 209.
Monday and Tuesday in Easter and Whitsun weeks, why observed, 543.
Montague (Bishop) on the sign of the Cross, 243.
Month's-mind, 454.
Mortuary and funeral celebrations. [Section xii, p. 159.]
"Most Highest," 383.

N

Name of Jesus, bowing at the, 197.
,,   why given in Baptism, 469.
Napkin and bason for the lavabo, 41.
Neuma. (See Pneuma.)
Nicene Creed, why reverences are made at "And was made man," 299.
,,   ,,   "worshipped and glorified," 299.
,,   sign of the Cross made at end of, 243.
Nones, one of the "hours of prayer," 582.
North (or Gospel) side of Altar, why service begun at, 287.
,,   ,,   ,,   why Gospel read at, 294.
,,   why Gospel read facing the, 224 (note).
Nunc Dimittis, usually sung after a High Celebration, 450.
,,   why incense not used at, 239 (note).

O

Oblation of the bread and wine, 310–12, 315.
Oblations, censing of the, 433.
,,   preparation of the, 427, 433.
,,   (veiling of the), what it represents, 313.

INDEX

"Obligation, days (or feasts) of," 388, 389.
Occasional Services, the. [Section xiii, p. 164.]
Octave of the Epiphany, why matrimony may be solemnized on, 484 (note).
Octaves, 175.
,, why observed, 176.
Offertory, what, and why so called, 300.
Office hymns (at Matins and Evensong), 250.
,, how arranged, 251.
,, ,, distinguished, 252.
,, ,, sung, 253.
,, Cranmer was anxious to have them translated, 250.
Oil, used in benedictions and consecrations, 130, 131.
,, of the sick, 131.
,, of catechumens, 131.
Orders (Holy) cannot be repeated, 473.
,, (Dissenters'), why not valid, 474.
,, higher, contain the lesser, 474 (note).
"Ordinary of the Season," 252.
Ordination, 135.
Oremus, or let us pray, why priest joins his hands at, 247.
Ornaments of the Church. [Section ii, p. 6.]
,, Ministers. [Section iii, p. 18.]
,, why set apart by a form of benediction, 110, 111.
O's (the), or greater Antiphons for the last eight days of Advent, 510.
O Sapientia, 510.
Ostension, 366.
Overall (Bishop), on the Eucharistic Sacrifice, 284.

P

Pall (funeral), its colour and ornamentation, 497.
,, why marked with the Cross, 495.
,, (of chalice), what, 313.
Palms (procession of), on the Sunday before Easter, 527.
Parisian tones, 211.
Paschal taper, 47, 541.
,, tide, kneeling formerly omitted in, 420.
Passion, Commemoration of (part of the Canon), 349.
,, the Eucharist a Sacramental, 393 (note).
,, Sunday, why so called, 524.
,, tide, 138, 524 (and note).
,, ,, its meaning, 139.

Passiontide, not to be confounded with Holy Week, 524 (note).
,, why pictures, etc., veiled during, 524.
Paten, 30.
* ,, formerly held by the Acolyte wrapped in the chalice-veil during certain parts of the service, 35.
Patron of the church, feast of the, 184.
Paul (S.), quotes from Liturgy of S. James, 6 (note).
,, the "cloke" which he left at Troas, 7 (note 1).
"Pax Domini," 392.
Penitential Psalms (the seven), why sung on Ash Wednesday, 522.
Pentecost, 138, 140.
,, colour of vestments at, 101, 104.
,, proper Psalms at, why chosen, 549.
,, why Baptism "solemnly" administered on the Eve, 472.
,, why marriages are restrained during, 484.
,, why the Monday and Tuesday are specially observed, 543.
Piscina, 42.
Planeta, why so called, 507.
,, why laid aside for the Gospel, etc., 507.
,, why worn in penitential seasons, 507.
Pneuma, what, 217.
,, its meaning, 219.
"Pointing" of the Psalms, 212.
Position of hands explained. (See Hands.)
Post-Communion, 382.
"Praise and thanksgiving (Sacrifice of)," 386.
Prayer of Humble Access, 340.
,, ,, why communicants only mentioned in, 341.
Preface, what, 329.
,, why chanted, 438.
,, why so called, 328.
"Preparation" of the oblations, 427, 433.
Presanctified, Mass of the, 536.
Prime, one of the "hours of prayer," 574-76.
Primer, contained services for the hours, 208.
,, contained dirge, or service of the dead, 554.
Principal ferias, 182.
Processional cross, 50.
,, ,, why in old English use one of wood painted red prescribed for Lent, and one of crystal for Eastertide, 266.

INDEX

Processions. [Section ix, p. 81.]
,, proper order of, 272.
,, symbolism of, 264.
,, when employed, 271.
,, why banners are used in, 267.
,, why headed by a cross, 265.
,, why place of honour is at the end, 269.
,, first religious service in Saxon England, a litany in, 270.
"Proper of Saints," 252.
,, of the Season, 252.
,, Prefaces, 330.
,, ,, when used, 331.
Psalm lxxxiv applied by spiritual writers to the Blessed Sacrament, 375.
*Psalms, lamps anciently kindled at the, 207.
,, why finished with a pneuma, 219.
*Psalter, anciently lights were kindled in honour of the, 207.
,, formerly sung through every week, 208.
,, Gregorian tones for the, 209.
,, of Salisbury, 577.
,, of S. Benedict, or monastic, 577.
,, pointing of the, 212.
,, ritual of the, 199–222.
Purple cassocks, 59.
,, one of the Church colours. (See Violet.)

Q

Queen Elizabeth's Latin Prayer Book allowed reservation, 396.

R

Red, one of the Church colours, 101.
,, why used at Whitsuntide, 101.
,, why used on feasts of martyrs, 101.
,, why used on feasts of the Holy Cross, 101.
,, (in the old English rite), why used on Sunday, 104, 105.
,, ,, why used on Ash Wednesday, 104, 105.
,, ,, why used on Maundy Thursday, etc., 104, 105.
Reproaches, what, and why sung on Good Friday, 538.
Reservation, 396.
,, preserved in Edward VI's first liturgy, 396.
,, allowed in Collegiate Churches by Queen Elizabeth's Latin Prayer Book, 396.

Responses, loud, out of character with Low Celebration, 324 (note 2).
Retable, 22.
Reverences (or bowings), why made at our Lord's Name, 197.
,, why made at *Gloria*, 196.
,, why made in Nicene Creed, 299.
,, why made in *Te Deum*, 233.
,, why made towards the Altar, 198.
Ridley (Bp.) on Eucharistic Adoration, 359.
Ring (in Matrimony), its meaning, 480.
,, why placed on fourth finger, 480.
,, why placed on left hand, 480.
"Ritualism" defined, 1.
Rochet, a variety of the surplice, 63, 279.
Rogation and Trinity Sunday, why marriage restrained between, 484.
,, days, what, 144.
,, ,, why so called, 145.
Rope, 109 (note).
Rulers of the Choir, 202-07.
,, why they sit at the Psalms, 205.
,, why they vary in number, 204.
,, why they wear copes, 205.
,, why the Choir has, 202.

S

"Sacrifice of praise and thanksgiving," 386.
,, (Eucharistic) not condemned by Article xxxi, 284.
,, ,, taught by best English divines, 284.
Sacring bell, what, and why rung, 52, 336 (and note), 369.
Salt, why mixed with blessed or "holy" water, 116.
Sanctus, what, and why so called, 333.
,, why the priest begins the intonation at the, 298.
,, why the deacon and subdeacon ascend at, 421.
,, why the people join in it, 334.
,, bell, what, and why rung, 52, 336 (and note).
Sandals, 109 (note).
Saturday (Holy), some ritualists hold that there should be no celebration on, 536.
Scapular, 109 (note).
Scarlet cassocks, 59.
Screen (Chancel), why surmounted by a cross, 13.
Scriptural character of symbolic worship, 4-6.
Seasons of the Christian year, 138.

INDEX

Seasons of the Christian year, their meaning, 139.
,, ceremonies peculiar to certain. [Section xiv, p. 175.]
,, the four Ember, 141, 142.
Sedilia, 24.
,, how used, and why, 27, 28.
Septuagesima, or greater Lent, 518.
,, colour of vestments in, 101, 104.
,, meaning of, 139, 518.
,, and Low Sunday, why marriages are restrained between, 484.
,, why "Alleluia" omitted in, 518.
,, why dalmatic and tunic laid aside, 506.
,, why *Te Deum* not used in, 229, 230.
Sequence, 424.
Server, why generally a boy, 281.
,, why he is first communicated at a Low Celebration, 375.
,, why Priest has a, 276.
"Service of Song," 190.
" ,, (this our bounden duty and)," 387.
Services, the occasional. [Section xiii, p. 164.]
Sext, one of the "hours of prayer," 581.
Shell, baptismal, 54.
Showbread (table of), a type of the Christian Altar, 347.
Shrove Tuesday, 520.
Side, chanting from side to, 192.
Sign of the Cross, 243, 244.
Silence, why the commemorations are made in, 320.
,, (why the Priest prays in) after the Consecration, 371.
Singing (antiphonal, or from side to side), 192.
Sisters, why buried in their proper habits, 499.
Solemn Celebration, what, 410.
,, ,, why incense used at, 415.
,, *Te Deum*. [Section vii, p. 78.]
"Solemnly" performed (why Baptisms are) on Easter and Whitsun Eves, 472.
,, (why the Litany is) at certain seasons, 261, 262.
"Song (Service of)," 190.
South (or Epistle) side of Altar, why Collect is said at, 292.
,, ,, why Epistle is read at, 294.
Sparrow (Bp.) on fasting Communion, 405 (note).
Species, each in the Blessed Sacrament has its own special grace, 363.

Spiritual Communion, 380.
Spoons, two sometimes used at the celebration of the Eucharist, 39.
Standing, why the Priest communicates, 374.
Stole, 75.
Stole, how worn in the Eucharist, 86.
,, its meaning, 87.
,, white, why used in the Churching of Women, 500.
,, why first a violet and then a white is used in administering Baptism, 467.
,, violet, why used in hearing Confessions, and in the Visitation of the Sick, 485.
,, not worn by subdeacon, 86.
,, worn by deacon over left shoulder only, 86.
,, ,, why, 87.
Stone or wood (why the Altar is made of), indifferently, 347.
Subdeacon, dress of the, 92–94.
,, why a Priest frequently acts as, 474 (note).
,, why he ascends at the Creed and *Gloria in Excelsis*, 421.
,, why he does not read the Epistle in the planeta, 507.
,, why he lays aside his tunic in preaching, 430.
,, why he reads the Epistle, 422.
,, why he stands below the deacon, 421.
"Suffice (it shall)," 307.
Sundays, how distinguished, 173.
Super-altar, 22 (and note).
Super-frontal, 22.
,, why generally red, 23.
Surplice, 56, 57, 60.
,, its meaning, 57.
Sursum Corda. (See "Lift up your hearts.")
Symbolic worship, how God is glorified by, 3.
,, scriptural character of, 4–6.
,, enforced by ecclesiastical history, 8.
Symbols, why employed in Divine Worship, 2.

T

Table, why the Altar is called the Lord's, 346.
,, Holy, the Altar so called in the Eastern Church, 347.
,, ,, Jewish Altar so called, 346.
Table, Holy, and heathen altars, 346.
Taper (Paschal), 47, 541.

INDEX

* Taper at Baptism, 471.
Tapers (funeral), 496.
Taylor (Bp.), on communicating fasting, 405.
,, on Eucharistic Adoration, 359.
Te Deum sung "solemnly" by way of thanksgiving. [Section vii, p. 78.]
,, why incense not then "offered," 258, 259.
,, why used on Epiphany Eve, 231.
,, why used in Whitsun Ember week, 231.
,, why *Gloria* is not added, 232.
,, why not used in Advent, 229.
,, why not used in Ember seasons, 229.
,, why not used in Lent, 229.
,, why not used on Vigils, 229.
* *Tenebrae*, 533.
Terce, one of the "hours of prayer," 578–580.
Ter Sanctus, what, and why so called, 333.
,, why people join in it, 334.
,, why Priest joins his hands at, 337.
Tertullian on funeral celebrations, 452.
Thirty-first Article does not condemn the word Mass, nor the primitive doctrine thereof, 284.
This is the Day (antiphon at Easter), why sung in place of hymn, 541.
"This our bounden duty and service," 387.
Three Hours' Agony (Devotion of) on Good Friday, 540.
Thurible, 48.
Tippet (choral), 73.
Title of the Church, feast of the, 184.
Tones (Ambrosian), 211.
,, (Gregorian), what, 209.
,, ,, how used, 210.
,, (Parisian), 211.
Tonus Peregrinus, or the eighth irregular tone, 209.
Tract, the, 425.
Trent (Catechism of), at one with Art. xxviii, 360 (note).
"Trine" (or threefold) immersion in Baptism, 470.
Trinity season, 138.
,, its meaning, 139.
,, colour of vestments in, 101, 104.
,, why it comes at the end of the year, 555.
,, Sunday, why marriages can be solemnized on, 484 (note).
Triptych, 51.

Tuesday (Monday and) in Easter and Whitsun weeks, why
   observed, 543.
Tunic, 92.
   ,,   why laid aside in preaching, 430.
   ,,   why not laid on the Altar, 430.
   ,,   why not worn in penitential seasons, 95, 506.
   ,,   why resumed on Maundy Thursday, 509.
   ,,   why resumed on Mid-Lent Sunday, 508.
   ,,   why resumed on third and fourth Sundays in Advent,
        508.
Twelvemonth's-mind, 453.
Twenty-eighth Article does not forbid the worship of Christ in
   the Eucharist, 360.

U

Unction, or anointing of the sick, 486.
Unleavened bread, why used by Western Church, 308.
"Use" of Salisbury or Sarum, 577.
   ,,   monastic, 577.

V

Veil (chalice), what, and why used, 34, 286.
Veiling of pictures, etc., in Passiontide, 524.
   ,,   Blessed Sacrament, 381.
   ,,   the oblations, what it represents, 313.
Venite, 199.
Versicles and Collect, why the Priest should stand at, 248.
Vespers. (See Evensong.)
   ,,   (first) of a feast, its mystical meaning, 165, 167.
   ,,   one of the "hours of prayer," 584-88.
Vestments in general. [Section iii, p. 18.]
   ,,   colour of, explained, 100-05.
   ,,   lights and incense always used in Christian worship, 8.
   ,,   the Eucharistic, 76-94.
   ,,   ,,   why worn, 77.
   ,,   ,,   their origin, 78.
   ,,   why special are assigned to the Eucharist, 77.
Viaticum, 488.
Vigils, 146.
   ,,   what they represent, 146
   ,,   colour of vestments on, 101, 104.
   ,,   why *Te Deum* not used on, 229.
Violet, one of the Church colours, 101.
   ,,   why used in Advent, Lent, etc., 101.

INDEX

Violet, why used for Bishop's cassock, 59.
,, stole, why used at Baptisms, 467.
,, ,, why used in the Visitation of the Sick, 485.
,, ,, why used in hearing confessions, 485.
Virgin, Feasts of the Blessed, 153.
,, ,, why white is used on, 101.
,, Saints who are not martyrs, why white is used on feasts of, 101.
Vocal and mental prayer, 320.

W

Wafer or unleavened bread, 308, 309.
Washing of hands or *Lavabo*, 314.
* ,, of the Altars on Maundy Thursday, 534.
Water, "holy" or blessed, 112–17.
,, why mixed with the wine in the Eucharist, 304, 305.
,, why blessed before being put into the chalice, 306.
,, why not blessed in mortuary celebrations, 464.
We do not presume. (See "Prayer of Humble Access.")
White, one of the ecclesiastical colours, 101.
,, stole, why used at Baptisms, 467.
,, ,, why used at Churching of Women, 500.
,, vestments, why used in solemnizing Matrimony, 475.
,, ,, in the funerals of infants, 498.
,, why Altar vested in on Maundy Thursday, 532.
Whit Monday and Tuesday, why observed, 543.
Whitsun Day, proper Psalms for, why chosen, 549.
Whitsun Ember Week, why *Te Deum* is said in, 231.
,, Eve, why Baptism "solemnly" administered on, 472.
Whitsuntide, 138, 139.
,, colour of vestments in, 101, 104.
,, why marriages are restrained during, 484.
Widow (why a) "plights her troth" with covered hand, 478.
Wine (in the Eucharist), why mixed with water, 304, 305.
Women (holy), not martyrs, why white is used on feasts of, 101.
Wood, why Altar sometimes made of stone, and sometimes of, 347.
Wren (Bishop) was wont to elevate the consecrated Sacrament, 367.

Y

Y-Cross on chasuble, its meaning, 91.
Year's-mind, or anniversary of a departed person, 453.
Yellow, how and why employed in old English rite, 104, 105.

www.ingramcontent.com/pod-product-compliance
Lightning Source LLC
Chambersburg PA
CBHW060123170426
43198CB00010B/1011